D0146183

TWAYNE'S

RULERS AND STATESMEN OF THE WORLD

SERIES

Hans L. Trefousse, Brooklyn College
General Editor

MARIA THERESA

(TROW 18)

Maria Theresa

By WILLIAM J. McGILL, JR.
Washington and Jefferson College

Twayne Publishers, Inc. :: New York

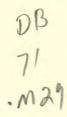

To

My Parents

Preface

M. S. ANDERSON, IN HIS EXCELLENT SURVEY *Europe in the Eighteenth Century*, asserts, "At their highest level the internal politics of the European States were the politics of monarchy, of monarchy which was usually powerful, and sometimes all-powerful." The eighteenth century marks that point in time when the states of Europe had been centralized, but were not fully bureaucratized. Thus the biographies of the monarchs and the histories of the reigns are in many instances identical. This is especially true for Central and Eastern Europe. Indeed, it may be impossible to write a "biography" of the likes of Frederick II, Catherine II, or Maria Theresa. At least the biographical literature in English recounting the lives of these monarchs has more dross than substance.

Maria Theresa poses an especially difficult problem for the biographer, because, unlike most of her fellow monarchs in the mid-eighteenth century, she was not an extraordinary personality possessed of Gargantuan vices, touched by madness, or gifted with spectacular virtues. She was devout and moral, steadfast and brave, but these virtues are the stuff of homilies, not of exciting biographies. Much of the biographical literature about her is little better than sentimental evocation of these virtues. Until quite recently, if one had to sum up the view of Maria Theresa which emerges from English-language biographies, the summary would read something like this: "She was really very nice even though she was an Austrian and a Catholic." In the last few years, however, several works have appeared which are worthy of note.

Robert Pick's *Empress Maria Theresa. The Earlier Years, 1717-1757* (New York, 1966) is a sometimes brilliant, sometimes clouded portrait of the young queen done in bold strokes. Still, the view is quite conventional and the work does not make use of the results of contemporary scholarship. Edward Crankshaw's *Maria Theresa* (London, 1969) provides a lucid and striking evocation of Theresian Austria which demonstrates both an awareness of the published sources and a sensitive appreciation for the subject—as well as the skills of a professional writer. Crankshaw is at his best describing the court life, but his interpretation of Maria Theresa proves the possibility of being sympathetic without being sentimental. His judgments of some of her advisers are overdrawn and his understanding of Maria Theresa's foreign policy is typically English, but he provides the best English-language biography to date. C. A. Macartney's *Maria Theresa and the House of Austria* (London, 1969) is a concise introduction to the ruler and her reign. Macartney brings to his subject an understanding honed by a long and thorough study of Habsburg history. Consequently, the interpretation is judicious though the leanness of the prose makes it appear oversimplified at times. Macartney provides a pen-and-ink sketch as opposed to Crankshaw's oil portrait and Pick's unfinished pastel.

Crankshaw observes, "Nobody close to her had the least understanding of the complexities of her make-up" (p. 103). The problem exists for her biographers as it did for her contemporaries. Having given this warning, I will not now declare that I have succeeded where others have failed. The purpose of this volume, simply put, is to provide a brief introduction to the current historical understanding of Maria Theresa and her reign. To accomplish this purpose, I have focused attention on the question of authority, that is, on the question, "Did Maria Theresa actually rule in her lands and was she therefore responsible for the achievements (and failures) of the monarchy?" This is obviously a rhetorical question, intended to provide a unifying theme while introducing the reader to the results of recent research. But it is not an arbitrary question, for it is the question which best integrates all that we know of Maria Theresa. What a person is cannot be distinguished from what he does, from his relationships with other people. The exercise of authority and the particular conception of that authority thus ultimately personify Maria Theresa.

The reign itself can be divided into three parts: the crisis of succession, 1740-1748; the reforming of the monarchy, 1748-1765; and the co-regency with Joseph, 1765-1780. The bulk of the important recent scholarship on Theresian Austria has concerned administrative reforms, social and economic policies, and the background to Joseph's religious policies. Therefore it has dealt primarily with the last two phases of the reign. By emphasizing

Preface

the question of authority, however, it is possible to comprehend the basic continuity of her reign as well as to appreciate better the role Maria Theresa played in Habsburg and European history. (The term "Austria," obviously an anachronism, is used here to refer to the Habsburg monarchy generally and is usually employed in contexts referring to attitudes or actions of the government. Where particular provinces or parts of the monarchy are omitted from consideration, the exclusion is explicitly made. Similarly, when an attitude or action is limited to specific provinces, they are named.)

I have intentionally minimized the scholarly apparatus. Thus, footnotes are limited to citing sources of direct quotations, supplying bibliographical references of particular importance, or providing explanatory comments. The bibliography itself has been selected to provide the reader with a guide to further study, and by no means is it indicative of the actual working bibliography. I believe I can say that in preparing this slim volume I have made an exhaustive survey of all appropriate secondary materials as well as the published primary sources.

Having tried to protect myself by defining the limited character of my intentions, I would add that this work is not simply a summary of other scholars' thoughts. While not pretending to provide a novel interpretation, I have attempted to set forth a view of Theresian Austria and its ruler based on my own analysis of what is known about that phase of Habsburg history. Thus I willingly accept responsibility for the conclusions here expressed.

I would, however, like to express my thanks to the following institutions and individuals: the Church Society for College Work, which provided a fellowship that permitted me to spend a summer in residence in Cambridge, Massachusetts; the staffs of the Vienna Archives, the Widener Library, and the university libraries at Michigan and Michigan State; Alma College, which partially subsidized the preparation of the manuscript; my father, who read and commented on several drafts; and last, but hardly least, my wife, Ellen, who typed and helped edit the manuscript.

W. J. M.

Alma, Michigan

Contents

Contents

Chronology

1711 Succession of Charles VI.
1713 Formulation of Pragmatic Sanction.
1717 Birth of Maria Theresa.
1733- War of the Polish Succession. Francis Stephen deprived of
1735 Lorraine.
1736 Marriage of Maria Theresa and Francis Stephen.
1737 Birth of Maria Elizabeth (1).
1738 Birth of Maria Anna.
1739 Sojourn in Florence.
1740 Birth of Maria Caroline (1). Death of Maria Elizabeth (1).
      Death of Charles VI and accession of Maria Theresa. Prussian
      invasion of Silesia.
1741 Birth of Joseph. Death of Maria Caroline (1). Coronation of
      Maria Theresa as Ruler of Hungary.
1742 Election of Charles Albert of Bavaria as Holy Roman Emperor.
      Birth of Maria Christina. Treaty of Breslau.
1743 Coronation of Maria Theresa as Queen of Bohemia. Birth
      of Maria Elizabeth (2). Treaty of Worms.
1745 Death of Charles VII. Election of Francis as Holy Roman
      Emperor. Birth of Karl Joseph. Treaty of Dresden.
1746 Birth of Maria Amalia. Conference of Breda. Alliance with
      Russia.
1747 Birth of Leopold.
1748 Birth and death of Maria Caroline (2). Treaty of Aix-la-
      Chapelle.
1749 State Conference. Haugwitz directs administrative reforms.
1750 Birth of Johanna Gabriella.
1751 Birth of Maria Josepha.
1752 Birth of Maria Caroline (3).
1753 Kaunitz named State Chancellor.
1754 Birth of Ferdinand.
1755 Birth of Marie Antoinette.
1756 Birth of Maximilian. Treaty of Versailles with France. Prussian
      invasion of Saxony initiates Seven Years' War.
1757 Second Treaty of Versailles with France.
1761 Revision of Haugwitzian system. Death of Karl Joseph.
1762 Death of Johanna. Dissolution of Russian alliance.
1763 Treaty of Hubertusburg.

1765   Further revision of Administration. Death of Francis. Joseph
       made Co-regent and elected Holy Roman Emperor.
1767   Death of Josepha.
1768   Outbreak of Russo-Turkish War and intensification of Polish
       crisis.
1769   Occupation of Spisz.
1770   Incorporation of Spisz.
1772   First partition of Poland.
1773   Expulsion of Jesuits.
1774   Revision of State Council. Beginning of peasant disturbances
       in Bohemia.
1775   Robot Patent.
1777- Bavarian Succession crisis.
1778
1780   Death of Maria Theresa.

CHAPTER I

The Heiress and Her Inheritance

IN 1741 HABSBURG FORTUNES HAD REACHED THEIR NADIR. AUSTRIA stood alone in Europe. Threatened by a coalition of her arch-enemies and forsaken by her "natural" allies, the young queen, Maria Theresa, who had succeeded Charles VI as head of the House of Habsburg in October, 1740, could not even be certain of the loyalty of the dynastic lands. Ironically, this power whose· rise to prominence had been summarized by the maxim, "others fight, but you, O happy Austria, marry," was hurled into crisis by the failure of the male succession.

The possibility of this hiatus was not unforeseen: it had in fact dominated the reign of Charles VI (1711-1740) who sought to offset the danger through guarantees embodied in the Pragmatic Sanction. Referring back to the Pact of Mutual Succession which he had made in 1703 with his brother Joseph (subsequently Joseph I [1705-1711]), Charles formulated the Sanction before the Privy Council in 1713. The Sanction reasserted the rule of primogeniture in Charles' line, but provided that should he die without male issue, the rights of succession would pass to his daughters. Should they die without heirs, the rights would revert to Joseph's daughters and their heirs, and, secondarily, to the daughters of Leopold I. Though the Habsburg monarchy remained a congeries of diverse dominions, the principle of indivisibility which the Sanction proclaimed was a critical step in the strengthening of the central government. No less important than the general principle were the results of the individual negotiations between Charles and his dominions to gain their acceptance of the Sanction. The agreements thus reached helped to delineate further the structure of the monarchy. In particular, Hungary's approval (1721-1722) underlined the unique position of that land within the monarchy. Equally important, Charles' desire to have the other states of Germany and Europe recognize the Sanction's validity became the central aim of his foreign policy.[1] Prince Eugene of Savoy warned the emperor that the best guarantees were a strong army and a full treasury, but the warning was not heeded. When Charles died, he bequeathed a treasury drained by a constant flow of subsidies, a skeleton army without the resources to expand and led by tired, aging generals; and a hatful of treaties—at a time when kings and princes viewed all guarantees "like works in filigree, more to satisfy the eye than to be of any use."[2]

The crisis confronting the House of Habsburg in the years 1740-1742 was a climactic one for that dynasty's past and future glory. The territorial resolution of the crisis set the framework for the creation of a German state that would ultimately exclude the Habsburgs and their lands while the accompanying internal stress both stimulated the reforms that transformed the monarchy into a modern state and perpetuated the critical weaknesses that finally culminated in its dissolution. Thus Austria's durability and her eventual mortality were both intricately related to this moment of crisis and the period of recovery which followed. Both in turn are bound to the reign of Maria Theresa, the mere girl who succeeded Charles VI.

Alfred von Arneth, the prolific nineteenth-century historian of Theresian Austria whose ten-volume biography remains the standard reference for the life of Maria Theresa, reported that little was known of her youth.[3] Another century of historical research has hardly added to our store of knowledge about those early years.[4] This veil of obscurity is not surprising, however, for no one assumed that the young archduchess would one day rule in her father's stead.

We do know a great deal about her birth. Charles VI desired a son, and because each moment in the life of an heir to the House of Habsburg was well worth recording we have a clear knowledge of Vienna's anxious wait in May, 1717. In 1716 Empress Elizabeth Christina had given birth to a son, but the expected, the longed-for, heir had soon died. Now the empress was confined again: the hope must now be fulfilled. On the morning of May 13 sometime before eight o'clock the child was born—a girl. Charles could not avoid showing his disappointment, but that disappointment was not yet final, for both he and his queen were young and healthy; a son might yet be born and in the meantime no one would regret the birth of an archduchess.

She would be brought up to fulfill the role expected of a Habsburg archduchess, to be a suitable wife for a great prince.

We know also a great deal about the baptism of the newborn which occurred that same evening, for to the Most Holy Catholic dynasty the sacramental act of Christian initiation was a matter of significance, even for an archduchess. Further, the ceremonial aspect of the occasion possessed a social significance that would guarantee a minute accounting of the event in the diaries and letters of those in attendance. The infant was baptized Maria Theresia Walburga Amalia Christina in a font containing five drops from the River Jordan and a "thorn from the crown of Christ." Various accounts of the ceremony pointedly refer to one aspect of the proceedings, the secondary position accorded to the daughters of Charles' brother and predecessor, Joseph I (1705-1711). Though Charles had not yet abandoned hope for a son, the protocol of the baptismal ceremony underlined the essence of the settlement, embodied in the Pragmatic Sanction, which gave precedence to Charles' daughters.

Aside from the events of May 13 our knowledge of Maria Theresa's youth is limited to two matters, both, however, of great importance: her education and her courtship. It is indicative of Charles' state of mind that while he worked so hard to prepare his lands for the undesirable eventuality of a female succession—by 1725 much of his energy was devoted to seeking guarantees for the Pragmatic Sanction—he did so little to prepare the young archduchess for the role she was to assume. Her education was a haphazard affair aimed at preparing her to be the wife of a prince rather than to rule. Perhaps this course was the better, for had she known the problems which would confront her she might well have been incapable of dealing with them. Her education lacked factual information and political instruction; it nevertheless instilled in her a sense of dignity and mission.

Carl Burckhardt has called Maria Theresa a child of the baroque and the last bearer of the Counter Reformation world view.[5] There have been numerous attempts to capture the spirit of the baroque—and there have been many disputes as to its real nature. In its most universal definition, the baroque is seen as a spiritual force which emanated from all aspects of social, cultural, political, and economic life, thus from the Jesuits, from the new cognition, from Machiavellianism and from Mercantilism.[6] The attempt to create so broad an analogy has been criticized, but even if it fails the attempt does manifest a crucial element of the age: the world was shuddering with a striving and a tension created by the continuation of great struggles and the emergence of great doubts. Maria Theresa was not brought up in a placid world, but in a world in which tradition and change, restoration and revolution, were in conflict. For Austria the baroque was particularly marked by the re-affirmation of Roman Catholicism and the growth of royal power and in that regard Maria Theresa was indeed "a child of the baroque."

She had numerous tutors: from Marinoni, who instructed her in mathematics, to the Jesuits, Michael Pachter and Franz Xaver Vogel, who instructed her in the faith; or the Countess Charlotte von Fuchs, in whose hands the general supervision of Maria Theresa's education was placed. But more important than the list of names is the substance of her education. The instruction she received was varied and there is little indication that much concern was placed on depth of knowledge or under-standing.

Her own interests and talent in art and music influenced the course of study. She learned Latin—the official language of Hungary—and a smattering of French and Spanish. In later life she often spoke and wrote in French because her true native language was the dialect of Vienna which was difficult for many non-Viennese to understand. She also possessed an excellent command of Italian, for her father was especially fond of that language. The Italian influence was more than linguistic. The musical background was distinctly Italian. Bach was not played in Vienna and Handel, to whom Joseph I had been partial, was replaced by the more southern tastes of Charles. As early as 1724 the young archduchess performed in a musical drama by Zeno, and regularly thereafter she and her sister, Maria Anna, entertained the court. Even in later life Maria Theresa would sometimes sing Italian arias to small groups. Further, the skills of artifice she developed in these family dramas were not without use to her as queen.

The lilting quality of Italian poetry and music provides an accurate reflection of the spirit of her youth. Though the narrow regimen of Spanish etiquette ruled the court, the family circle was free from such restrictions. "Reserl," as Maria Theresa was called, contributed a lively and energetic presence to a ménage more reminiscent of a Viennese burgher's household than of the other German courts. The sumptuous family entertainments in which Charles delighted and which he readily provided gave a color and intensity to the intimacies of family life that makes them appear in our day as part of a play within a play. But the gaiety of life was controlled by the persistent demands of piety.

"Baroque piety" has a peculiarly theatrical character.[7] It is a style meant to provide an external expression of the inner spiritual life. For both contemporaries and subsequent commentators there lurked the danger that style would be mistaken for substance. There was false piety, but baroque piety was not mere charade; it was the reflection of a deep and turbulent belief. The brilliant colors and elaborate decoration of the churches and shrines seem best suited to the expression of joy, but there was a gloomier strain, a persistent awareness of mortality and judgment. Maria Theresa's religious training instilled in her a full measure of faith, and piety became for her a natural attribute. In her youth it gave her meaning; in her mature years it gave her strength, then comfort. In times of joy it sobered her; in times of sorrow it sustained her.

With some regret many biographers, especially those who have written in English, have noted that the Jesuits provided much of the formal instruction which Maria Theresa received, and that the principal effect of their ministrations was to increase her piety. Indeed, Jesuit fathers were important, but were not the exclusive authors of her education; and the importance of religious policies in the last half of her reign made her piety a matter of enormous consequence. Furthermore, to her tutors Maria Theresa owed her conception of the dignity which she was to assume and her understanding of the historical plane on which she had to move. In this regard, Gottfried Philipp Spanagel, the court historian and curator of the court library, who was explicitly appointed as her history tutor, was probably the most influential.

Spanagel's own view of the political order has been characterized as a secularistic but not an Enlightenment view. His own inclinations were antipapal and his insistence on the preeminence of the monarchy naturally followed. Though the theory of divine right monarchy was not the key to his monarchial conception, the scope of monarchial authority within the state could hardly have been greater, and he has been called a "secular Bossuet."[8] It would be inaccurate to credit him with being a profound political theoretician, the philosopher of the Theresian monarchy. The notebooks he assembled to guide his young student are dotted with such questions as "How much longer did Methusalah live than Adam?" and "Which Persian king was killed in an ashbin?" Despite these minutiae Spanagel spoke largely in generalities, in the abstract. There is no indication that he ever made concrete proposals of policy. In her later life Maria Theresa read very little history, most of her reading being devoted to official dispatches and books of meditation, and she was more at home with the history of classical antiquity than with the history of her own dynasty. Yet Spanagel's stress on certain simple elements of the nature of power had great influence on Maria Theresa's approach to her tasks. Specifically, he emphasized the proper "historical" virtues; the right to rule, not only of monarchs in general, but of queens in particular; and the relationship between the ruler and the church.

Among his favorite texts was the *Cyropaedia* of Xenophon, especially the closing portions in which the great King Cyrus, on his death bed, assembles his sons, his friends, and his chief advisers for a last word of advice. To begin, Cyrus emphasizes the right of the eldest-born to succeed him. At the same time he insists that the kingdom cannot be protected by the sword alone, but depends on the aid of friends, of whom the most natural are the brothers of the heir. He warns Cambyses that loyal hearts do not grow untended, rather faithfulness must be won. Indeed, his last words of advice are, "Show kindness to your friends, and then you shall have it in your power to chastise your enemies." Cyrus—and Spanagel—also insisted on the necessity of reverencing the gods to whom everything is owed and in whom all power ultimately rests. No man rules but that god wills it so. After the gods the ruler must reverence all men, for a monarch does not rule in darkness but in the eyes of men, and the confidence of men is required that the ruler might maintain his power. In this and in all things, "let history teach you, and there is no better teacher."

An equally significant text was the account of the Investiture Controversy of the eleventh century, in which Spanagel concentrated his views on the relationship between monarch and church. The explanation of this critical event presented to the young archduchess was quite one-sided in its contrast between the intentions of pope and emperor. The misfortunes of the monarch were explicitly attributed to the excessive ambitions of Gregory VII, while Henry IV's efforts to limit the temporal power of the papacy were depicted as his most noble purpose. The medieval emperors were exonerated from any accusation of perfidy on the basis that the duplicity of the popes dissipated whatever obligations of obedience the emperors might have incurred. Thus Spanagel rejected the concept of papal over-lordship not on the principles of natural and constitutional law, but with the argument that the popes themselves had dissolved the old relationship by their immoralities. He reiterated the superior position of the imperium by asserting that the renunciation was not subject to the concurrent approval of the electoral princes.

The freedom of the monarch from ecclesiastical interference was thus clearly affirmed and the royal prerogative asserted. At the same time, however, there was no trace of Josephinism in Spanagel's lessons. Nevertheless, given Maria Theresa's basic piety, had her historical training been pro-papal, or at least more objective, she would not have been so trustful of such men as Kaunitz in matters relating to the church.[9] On the other hand, had Spanagel's views contradicted the general tenor of Maria Theresa's broader education in the nature of the monarchy, they would have had little effect and less importance. In fact the rigid pro-imperial interpretation of the medieval struggle for right order reaffirmed a generalized inclination toward the state-church idea which already had wide appeal in Germany.

Even after 1725 when the possibility of having a male heir had largely dissipated, Charles seemingly could not accept the obvious eventuality of Maria Theresa's succession. For all his attention to guaranteeing the Pragmatic Sanction, Charles may still have clung to the elusive hope that some other solution might yet emerge. Indeed, the moment of truth seemed remote, for he was still relatively young and in good health. He would certainly live long enough for the young archduchess to be safely married to some worthy prince and for an heir to be born. The most likely "worthy prince" was Francis Stephen of Lorraine. As early as June, 1722, Duke Leopold of Lorraine-had broached with Prince Eugene of Savoy the subject of a marital alliance between his eldest son Clemens and Maria Theresa.

Prince Eugene apparently approved the idea. Even though Charles VI did not openly endorse the project, he encouraged Leopold to send Clemens to the Viennese court where "I will be his father and the prince will be my son, so openly will I converse with him at all times."[10] The House of Lorraine had been a staunch ally and an actual union promised to strengthen still further the Habsburg position on the Rhine, a necessity for the dynasty's holdings in the Low Countries. Further, the reports Charles received about the ducal heir were most favorable. He was clearly disappointed when Prince Clemens died of the small-pox in June, 1723, before reaching Vienna. After the initial shock, however, Leopold concluded that his second son, Francis Stephen, who would now succeed to all the claims of his brother, might aspire to the hand of Archduchess Maria Theresa. While Charles was somewhat hesitant, apparently on the basis of the less than favorable reports he had heard of Francis, Prince Eugene continued to favor the alliance and so the emperor again expressed his willingness to have the ducal heir come to the court of Vienna. As yet such a marriage was not irrevocably bound to the problem of the headship of the dynasty, for in 1723 hope for a son and heir still persisted.

On August 10, 1723, the fifteen-year-old heir to the duchy of Lorraine presented himself to the emperor.[11] He would remain at the Habsburg court until March 4, 1729, when at the death of his father he returned to assume control of his hereditary lands. In the interim his education and training were ultimately the concern of Charles VI, and the bond of affection between himself and his future bride was rooted. Despite initial hesitation Charles was quickly pleased with the youth, not a little because of his enthusiasm for and talents in the hunt, Charles' own favorite diversion. Duke Leopold feared that too much time was spent hunting, but the constant contact with the emperor which the chase allowed compensated for his misgivings. In more intellectual pursuits Francis proved less apt. Though intelligent, he lacked the desire to apply himself to the stricter tasks of education. Despite constant encouragement from his father and the emperor, and the appointment of special tutors, Francis remained more devoted to the gentlemanly skills of fencing, hunting, and dancing. Even so, he was a pleasurable companion for Charles and a captivating subject of admiration for the young archduchess.

A general understanding that prevailed that when the time came the young couple would marry—Charles in his letters to Duke Leopold consistently referred to his hopes for a "closer union" between their families—but no formal obligation was established. Consequently, the possibility of a marital alliance with the Habsburg heiress continued to entice other monarchs. The daughters of Joseph I, the wives of the electors of Saxony and Bavaria, were both anxious that a match might be made for their eldest sons and both clearly had a certain voice in the inner circle of the dynasty in the person of their mother, the Dowager Empress Amalia. Both candidates were much younger than Maria Theresa, but that was seldom a consideration in arranging such marriages. A marital union with Bavaria was especially tempting because the merging of the Wittelsbach and Habsburg lands would have greatly strengthened the German character and power base of the dynasty. Reportedly when Maria Theresa heard of one of these proposals, she threw a tantrum and refused to eat for several days. Though probably apocryphal, the story illustrates Maria Theresa's ready acceptance of the idea that one day she would marry the cavalier from Lorraine.

Maria Theresa was six when Francis Stephen arrived at the imperial court. A born charmer with an instinctive knowledge of how to please others, Francis could hardly help but delight the blue-eyed child. Even the slightest attention from so gallant a young cavalier almost inevitably nurtured a childish love in Reserl's heart—and he, after all, knew why he had come to Austria. Charles' own obvious affection for Francis, in whose presence he found some solace for his paternal disappointments, strengthened Maria Theresa, for in adoring the one she might think to please the other. In 1727 Maria Theresa fell ill and at first smallpox was feared, but happily she recovered. Shortly thereafter Francis too sickened, recovering only after a long convalescence. This near double tragedy seemed to cement the bond between the two young people. Maria Theresa's own childish affirmations of love now found a friendly ear in Countess Fuchs, her new governess. Not to be outdone, Empress Elizabeth also encouraged her daughter to think fondly of the Lorrainer.

The mounting certainty that Maria Theresa would indeed succeed her father, however, made the proposed marital alliance less and less attractive, at least to some of Charles' counselors. Maria Theresa later remarked that her father had not been entirely deaf to their pleadings.[12] Charles' actual intentions remain quite unclear; in this matter as in others he seems rather to have wished to avoid rendering an irrevocable decision than to have seriously pursued an alternative. Thus Charles probably never intended to accept a proposed marriage between his eldest daughter and Don Carlos of Spain, a proposal rumored near acceptance in 1726, nor a subsequent suggestion that she marry Frederick of Prussia. In March, 1729, when Francis returned to Lorraine to assume the ducal title he was still the only identifiable candidate for the marriage.

Francis left Vienna with the greatest reluctance for, having inherited his father's ambition that Habsburg and Lorraine be one, he feared lest he be forgotten. He need not have feared, for prior to his departure Maria Theresa made clear her great affection for him and during his absence contact was maintained, though indirectly. At Christmas in 1730 Charles anonymously presented to Maria Theresa a miniature of Francis; Countess Fuchs duly reported the warmth of her reaction to both emperor and duke. Francis' tour of European courts in 1731 bristled with significance: he restricted his visits to courts already adhering to the Pragmatic Sanction, in particular visiting three imperial electors, the Kings of England (Hanover) and Prussia and the Archbishop of Mainz, and wherever he went Charles' friendly recommendation preceded him. In 1732 he returned to Vienna. The moment for a public declaration seemed at hand: instead, Charles despatched Francis to Pressburg as *Statthalter* of the Kingdom of Hungary. Charles' unwillingness to commit himself further was characteristic: he vacillated not because he wished to pursue another course, but because to decide, to act, was to make a final resolution. And, after all, the archduchess was still young: there was no hurry.

The outbreak of the War of the Polish Succession in 1733 introduced still another complication. The demands made by the French for the concession of the duchy of Lorraine to Stanislaus Leszczynski, demands supported by the course of events in the war, raised the obvious problem whether it was politically wise to marry the heiress of the House of Habsburg to a duke without a duchy. By 1735 the emperor had suffered serious losses in Germany and in Italy. His principal advisers were warning him that there would be little possibility of enforcing the Pragmatic Sanction. The course of action which was proposed called for the division of the dynastic lands. Those lands which had formerly been held by the now extinct Spanish branch of the House of Habsburg would be held by Maria Anna—and she would be married to Don Carlos of Spain. All other lands of the dynasty would be bequeathed to Maria Theresa and she would be married to a German prince. Specifically, Prince Eugene urged a union with the Bavarian electoral prince, who would then be elected King of the Romans, thus subsequently Holy Roman Emperor. In this way the dynasty could fulfill its German mission while avoiding the danger of a complete dismemberment of its own lands.

Meanwhile negotiations for the settlement of the War of the Polish Succession continued and the loss of Lorraine seemed inevitable. Charles was given the unhappy function of acquiring Francis' signature to the cession. Not surprisingly, he asked one of his ministers, Johann Christoph Bartenstein, to carry out the task, and Bartenstein, in his blunt and practical manner, is said to have informed Francis: "No cession, no archduchess." This incident has evoked the most saccharine responses from Maria Theresa's numerous sentimental biographers:

> In this cruel, brutal manner the finest courtship in the History of the House of Hapsburg was terminated. A real love affair, tender and sweet as a garden flower was bruised and crushed until all its romance oozed out, evaporated and vanished, leaving a devotion stripped of all its beauty and poetry. Charles VI, instead of graciously bestowing his daughter upon a pleading lover, tossed her across the counter to Francis of Lorraine, begging and urging him to accept her as the price of something sorely needed to save the dynasty.[13]

More to the point is the question why did Charles reject the far more realistic and favorable proposal for a marital union with Bavaria, a proposal strongly encouraged by Prince Eugene. The only answer admissible in the light of existing evidence is that Charles was unwilling to break the trust implied in his relationship with the House of Lorraine since 1723. As to the cession of Lorraine, the matter was not negotiable as was apparent when Charles attempted to convince the French that Francis should be allowed to retain Lorraine until the succession to Tuscany was opened and Francis' ducal title transferred there. Ultimately, Charles gave his consent to the marriage before the cession was signed.

That this "inhuman pressure" destroyed the love between
Maria Theresa and Francis is dubious to say the least. It was ever
true that her devotion to him was greater than his for her, if for
no other reason than that he was far more superficial both
temperamentally and intellectually than his bride. The loss of
Lorraine undoubtedly affected Francis because without his
patrimony he was unmistakably a dependent on the Habsburg
court and his self-esteem suffered accordingly. Still, the undis-
guised simplicity and intensity of Maria Theresa's love for him
more than compensated his masculine ego for this slight. It must
have been a far more brutal shock for him to discover after 1740
that his adoring wife would not, could not, defer to him the
responsibilities which were hers as the heiress of the House of
Habsburg. Furthermore, given Francis' character, one must
assume his subsequent peccadilloes had little to do with the
cession of Lorraine.

On February 12, 1736, the wedding took place in the court
church with the papal nuncio Domenico Passionei performing
the ceremony. After celebrations, foreshortened to two days by
the approach of Lent, the young couple journeyed to Maria Zell
to place their union under the protection of the Blessed Virgin.
Charles, at least, must have prayed earnestly for sons to be born
of this union.

The slender, doe-eyed archduchess had had her way, the
love match was made and the burdens of state seemed still a
remote responsibility. The next four years should have been the
happiest of Maria Theresa's life, for she was wife and lover of
her cavalier and thrice would bear him a child. Yet as the
luxuriant colors and intricate designs of baroque had their
shadows, her joy was laced with gloomy forebodings. The world
was too much with the young couple. The storm that would
break over the Habsburg dominions after 1740 gathered on the
horizon and ominous rumbles already sounded.

The succession problem required attention. The French refused
to allow Francis to remain in possession of Lorraine until Tuscany
fell vacant. Despite mutterings to the contrary he had no choice
but withdrawal: refusal meant war and war meant the danger
of losing Tuscany as well as Lorraine. The trade itself hardly
appealed to Francis. To lose his hereditary lands and then to be
made a duke on Habsburg sufferance, at that a duke in a duchy
where he must share authority with the nobility and the estates,

hardly seemed auspicious. Indeed, to idle about the Habsburg court until Tuscany called him was an abomination. Francis needed prestige. To be sure, as husband of Maria Theresa, Francis was the logical Habsburg successor to the title of Holy Roman Emperor, yet the logic was flawed: could the Habsburgs offer as candidate a landless duke? Charles fretted, but could not bring himself to press for the election of Francis as King of the Romans which would have secured the imperial succession. Instead, on May 4, 1736, Charles offered his son-in-law the governor-generalship of the Austrian Netherlands until he could occupy the Grand Duchy of Tuscany. Before the official declaration of this appointment was made, however, Austria was again at war, this time with Turkey.

On April 20, 1736, Prince Eugene of Savoy, the most dominant figure in Habsburg affairs since the beginning of the century, had died.[14] Though declining in both mental and physical powers, Eugene was still the wisest of Charles' advisers, and bereft of his wisdom, Charles stumbled into the war with Turkey despite the protests of his other ministers. In 1726 Charles had made an alliance with Russia as one step in his effort to guarantee the Pragmatic Sanction. Now Russia was demanding aid in her struggle with Turkey. Although Austria's obligation was not operative since the Russians had been the aggressor, the emperor responded because of the Pragmatic Sanction. Perhaps Charles was enticed also by the possibility of repeating the brilliant successes which Austria had enjoyed against Turkey under Eugene's generalship. Only this illusory hope could have prompted so extensive an intervention into the war at a time when royal finances were in such serious straits.

Amidst the mounting crisis Maria Theresa grew heavy with child and, on February 5, 1737, gave birth—to a daughter, Maria Elizabeth. No matter, the marriage was fertile and Charles still hearty. The emperor did hesitate to appoint Francis to the staff of Count von Seckendorf, who was to lead Austrian forces against Turkey, though Francis was eager for the opportunity. Enemy weapons, campaign illness, or mere accident posed too great a danger while Francis still had sons to father. Charles relented, however, for he, like Francis, understood that the surest means of strengthening the young duke's position was to let him bask in the glory of a successful military campaign.

The war proved a disappointment for the inexperienced and

overanxious young duke and an agony for his wife. Blame for
the early military failures fell squarely on Seckendorf: what, his
enemies at court asked, could one expect when a Protestant was
given command in a war against the infidel? Seckendorf was
relieved and placed under arrest and Francis succeeded him.
Almost simultaneously Charles announced that on those occasions
when he was not present, Francis would preside over meetings
of the Privy Conference. Austria was to have a new Eugene! But
too much was expected of the new command. Hampered by
illness and desertion, the difficulty of acquiring reinforcements,
and financial problems, the army could not pursue the war.
Francis, though zealous, lacked strategic sense as well as
experience and his chief adviser, Count Königsegg, the President
of the War Council, merely balanced Francis' impetuosity with
indecision, not wisdom. So eager to grasp the ring of fortune
which had eluded Seckendorf, Francis now found himself the
object of public scorn.

These were the loneliest, the bitterest days, of Maria Theresa's
life (at least until the years of her widowhood). Separated from
her beloved, she felt the anger toward Francis all around her,
yet was powerless to defend him. She prayed that the campaign
might make his reputation, yet feared it would only take his life.
Again pregnant, she was nervously happy about the new life
growing within her, for she was apprehensive of the reaction
if she bore another daughter—as she did, Maria Anna, born
October 6, 1738. The "blessed event" intensified anxieties at
court. Charles, having failed to continue the male line himself,
desperately desired that his daughter should reestablish it. He
could not restrain his disappointment and so grieved Maria
Theresa. Had she borne a son the rising antagonism toward
Francis might have abated, but instead it increased. The foreigner
could only breed daughters and lose battles! Maria Theresa
herself came under attack. Some among the nobility and the
populace even openly proposed that Charles' second daughter,
Maria Anna, should be married to the electoral prince of Bavaria
and the order of succession changed in her favor. When Bavarian
troops, returning to Munich from Hungary, passed through
Vienna, the people greeted them enthusiastically, shouting that
they soon would all be subjects of the same lord.

Reacting to this pressure, Charles decided to send the young
couple to Tuscany. Though some observers saw devious motives

in this action, Charles had no intention of altering the succession, but he recognized the dangers involved if Maria Theresa should become too unpopular before her accession. Exile to Florence would remove Maria Theresa and Francis from the center of the storm. Reluctantly they departed; arriving in Florence on January 20, 1739, they would leave just three months later never to return. The brief sojourn in Florence was not a happy time though the Florentines received them eagerly and in future years neither Maria Theresa nor Francis referred to those months. Maria Theresa was again with child and her younger daughter was ill. Despite the Italian orientation of her education, she felt herself a stranger in a foreign land, for the age of baroque had little touched Florence. Its glories were of the past and in the eighteenth century Florence was a backwater, a small provincial town in comparison with Vienna. Though Francis plunged into the business of ruling his duchy and at the very least established a bureaucratic structure which could govern in his absence, he still yearned for military glory. Happily removed from the baleful looks and dark innuendoes that had blighted her life at court, Maria Theresa forgot them and now wanted only to return to the familiar surroundings of Vienna. And in Vienna Charles fretted, now fearing that the absence of his heiress was more injurious to his hopes than her presence. Soon he recalled them.

Charles wisely did refuse Francis' desires for a return to the military campaign. And so his son-in-law was spared the abuse poured on the Austrian military as a result of the disastrous Peace of Belgrade by which Austria ceded that city and everything that she had acquired by the Treaty of Passarowitz (1697) except Temesvar. Charles dolefully wrote Bartenstein:

This year took many years off my life, to which only a few are left. God wills it so! He gives me the power to bear it, through it my sins are expiated, and where I am wanting it will serve as a correction and warning.[15]

The power to bear misfortune ebbed away. On January 12, 1740, Maria Theresa gave birth to her third child and third daughter, Maria Caroline. Charles interpreted this as punishment for his dynasty. The rumblings against Francis renewed and some said that Count Neipperg, the Austrian negotiator at Belgrade, had acted on orders from Francis. Then Maria Elizabeth, Charles' eldest and favorite granddaughter, died on June 6, 1740. Still,

Charles hesitated to act to guarantee Francis' election as King of the Romans. He knew that without that guarantee the inheritance of his well-loved daughter was not secure, yet he procrastinated.

In October he journeyed to Halbthurn to hunt, but fell violently ill from eating some spoiled food, perhaps a dish of mushrooms. On October 20, 1740, Charles died. The House of Habsburg was played out: only a girl was left.

CHAPTER II

Maria Theresa Defends Her Inheritance

IN THE EARLY 1730's MARIA THERESA WAS INTRODUCED TO THE councils of state as preparation against the time when she would succeed her father. There is no record that she had any decisive influence on his policies, but she clearly made an impression on those who observed her. Thomas Robinson, the English representative, remarked, "She is a princess of the highest spirit; her father's losses are her own. She reasons already; she enters into affairs; she admires his virtues, but condemns his mismanagement; and is of a temper so formed for rule and ambition as to look upon him as little more than her administrator."[1] The Venetian ambassador remarked that she possessed such spirit and temper that if one had to choose from all the women in the world he would identify her as the heiress to the Habsburg lands.[2] Already evident was that royal bearing, that steadfast conviction of her right and her duty, which preserved her and her monarchy in the first dark days of her reign. Carlyle's exuberance did not much mislead him when he exclaimed:

Most brave, high and pious-minded; beautiful too, and radiant with good nature, though of temper that will easily catch fire: there is, perhaps, no nobler woman then living. And she fronts the roaring elements in a truly grand feminine manner as if Heaven itself and the voice of Duty called her: "The Inheritances which my Fathers left me, we will not part with these. Death, if it so must be, but not dishonor. Listen not to that thief in the night!"[3]

Yet until the day following her father's death when, for the first time, she presided over a meeting of the Privy Conference, she remained a shadowy, elusive figure. The mere glimpses of her earlier life that biographers now provide, accurately reflect the perception of her contemporaries: few expected her to take up the reins of government so vigorously; most assumed

she would wear the ceremonial robes of authority, but Francis
would wield the scepter. She would transmit, but not exercise
power. What else could they assume: the annals of her dynasty
had no precedent for a woman ruler, let alone an active, dynamic
one. Furthermore, she had taken to bed on hearing of her
father's illness, prostrated by grief and perhaps by fear of what
confronted her. When the summons came, however, Maria
Theresa was equal to the task. She accepted her role not gladly,
but willingly, for though convinced that a woman's place was in
the home as wife and mother, she as firmly believed that God
had called her to her new station. Not desirous of power, she
was motivated by a deep sense of duty. Though again pregnant,
Maria Theresa hardly took the time to eat or to sleep as she
attempted to understand her new obligations and to exercise
her new responsibilities.

Among the treasures which the Vienna Archives have yielded
to historians are two memoranda which taken together compose
Maria Theresa's political testament.[4] She herself regarded them
as the summary of the problems which she had inherited from
her predecessors and those which would confront her successors.
The first memo she entitled, "Instructions composed because
of maternal concern for the special needs of my posterity which
will be considered in separate discussions according to their
importance." Almost half the first memorandum deals with two
topics: the condition of the monarchy at the time of her accession and the errors into which the monarchy had fallen under
her predecessors. (The other four topics she intended to discuss
were the measures taken during the war, the internal reforms
enacted after 1748, the consequences of these reforms for the
future, and the necessity of preserving internal order and of
proceeding wisely. Of these the only one she treated in detail
in the first memo was internal reform.) In her analysis of the
condition of the monarchy at the time of her accession, Maria
Theresa stressed two things: first, she lacked money, troops,
and advice, and, second, she had not been properly prepared
for her role. Lacking experience in dealing with her counselors,
she hardly knew where to begin. Significantly, she regretted not
only the scarcity of men and money, needs which had long been
apparent, but also the failure of her ministers to advise her.
She herself was quite specific in her opinions about these men,
whom she also had inherited, noting for example that while

Count Sinzendorf appeared willing to keep her informed, she did not have faith in him. Sinzendorf had been the chief adviser of Charles VI in the last years of his reign and seemed intent on occupying the same place of honor in the new reign. This very eagerness disturbed Maria Theresa and led her to depend more heavily on Count Starhemberg, though she readily admitted that he lacked the political insight of Sinzendorf. Bartenstein she disliked, for he had always seemed to be in the midst of the various intrigues directed against Francis. Uncertain as they were as to her intentions and her capacity, all the counselors played a waiting game and all were surprised, perhaps disappointed, when she showed herself so determined to rule as well as reign. Rather than concealing her inexperience she openly confessed it and requested that each member of the Privy Conference take it upon himself to inform her about everything within his competence that she needed to know. Her father's ministers were thus indispensable to her. She needed their knowledge and their experience and therefore they were retained. Given the dangers of the situation she inherited, it was necessary to take advantage of the continuity which their service provided.

The first task she took up had personal as well as dynastic significance: she set out to acquire the Holy Roman Imperium for Francis against the rival claims of Charles Albert of Bavaria. She had also to defend her landed inheritance from Bavarian claims. France, not Bavaria, seemed to offer the real threat, however, for Charles Albert could not act on either of his pretensions without French support, though the immediate danger from France was slight since the aging Cardinal Fleury still controlled French policy. While he sought to secure Charles Albert's election as emperor he had no desire to go to war and fully intended to respect the Pragmatic Sanction despite the urgings of a faction at the Versailles court led by the Count de Belle-Isle to seize the opportunity to cripple Habsburg power.[5] Maria Theresa regarded the imperium as inseparable from her inheritance; the desire to honor Francis intensified this conviction. Her attention fixed on the imperial prize, she failed to anticipate—no one did—and was rudely shaken by Frederick of Prussia's abrupt invasion of Silesia (December 23, 1740).[6]

Thus erupted the rivalry that would dominate Continental

politics for the next quarter century and German politics for the next century and a quarter. Under Frederick William (1713-1740), Prussian strength had increased rapidly, but Frederick William's passivity on the international front, his apparent willingness to defer to Habsburg leadership, had obscured this growth. For Frederick William the mere existence of the army he had so carefully created was sufficient; for Frederick, bursting with the energy and confidence of youth, the army was an instrument, valueless if not used. Prussia had a tenuous claim to Silesia but more to the point is Frederick's own admission:

Add to the previous considerations troops ever ready to act, my well-filled treasury and the vivacity of my character: these were the reasons I made war on Maria Theresa, Queen of Bohemia-Hungary.[7]

He did not long retain this brash belief in action for action's sake. The fright he received on the field at Mollwitz from where in mid-battle he fled—only to have his army triumph—quickly transformed this drive into a more calculating though hardly less aggressive statecraft. Characteristically, however, the incident of Mollwitz did not shake his firm self-assurance.

Prussia's sudden thrust shattered the nervous calm that prevailed in Europe. Now, not only was the Habsburg claim to the imperial title in jeopardy, but the continued existence of the dynasty itself was threatened. The wolf having struck, the vultures came. Fleury, still desirous of peace, could no longer restrain the hawks: France promised Charles Albert support for his claims and Belle-Isle journeyed to Frederick's camp. Frederick Augustus of Saxony, though suspicious of Prussia, refused Maria Theresa's urgent requests for aid, remaining neutral in anticipation of making territorial gains at her expense. George II of England feared that any commitment to Austria would endanger Hanover, and his chief minister, Robert Walpole, whose chief desire was to keep England out of war, quickly seconded him. English vacillation in turn determined the policy of Holland. Both sea powers aimed to reconcile Austria and Prussia.

Domestic harmony suffered as well. At the same time that he overran Silesia, Frederick offered to support Austria's imperial claims and guarantee her other lands in return for acceptance of his control of Silesia. Frederick made the offer directly to Francis and there are ample indications that Francis was receptive to the idea.[8] Maria Theresa, her sense of justice violated by Frederick's abrupt and deceitful action, angrily rejected any idea of negotiation with Prussia. Her refusal not only induced Frederick to sign an agreement with France (June 5, 1741), but it also demonstrated the character of the co-regency. She held the scepter tightly.

The year 1741 had begun bitterly for the young queen. On January 25 her youngest daughter, Maria Caroline, died, yet she had no time for personal grief. Frederick's attack had encouraged other claimants to Habsburg lands to press their demands. Maria Theresa's determined attitude in the face of these dangers had won her some support in her lands—the nobles of Bohemia and Moravia pledged recruits and money to the defense of the dynasty—but the possibility of a supporting alliance with another great power remained remote. The birth of Joseph, on March 13, 1741, momentarily dispelled the gloom. When the announcement was made Vienna exploded with joyous enthusiasm. At last a son and heir! The difficulties of past and present seemed trivial and a brighter future was promised. The once-maligned Francis was hailed as the "boymaker." Banners hung on every building and across every street. Indicative of the spirit that prevailed in Vienna was one streamer which defiantly proclaimed, "The enemy has lost his chance/For Austria now wears pants."[9] Festivities continued for a week, reaching a climax on the day of the baptism.

Everyone assumed the boy would be named after Maria Theresa's father, but shortly before the ceremony itself Maria Theresa informed her mother that during the pregnancy she had frequently invoked in prayer the aid of St. Joseph and so felt obligated to name her son Joseph. If the dowager empress was disappointed in this decision, the Viennese were delighted, for happy memories of the brief reign of Joseph I still lingered. The choice was symbolic in another way: Maria Theresa had made clear again the profoundly religious sense of duty which moved her and had asserted her conviction that she alone must finally decide what that sense of duty required.

Even at this moment she could not act with mere joy. The weight of her responsibilities prevented her from simply immersing herself in the delights of her family. Having taken up the burden, she was to find that her life could never again be quite the same. An individual might accept the roar of the crowd as sufficient, but as ruler Maria Theresa knew instinctively that without physical strength, public spirit was meaningless. Hardly pausing to enjoy the fruit of her labors, Maria Theresa continued her effort to consolidate control in her lands, an effort first centered on Hungary. In her dramatic appeal to the Magyars were revealed the singular qualities of this monarch.

Hungary had acknowledged the Pragmatic Sanction and had accepted Francis as governor, but the tensions which had flared so violently early in the century still existed: the enemies of the dynasty certainly expected that they would find support in the land of the Magyars. In fact, however, those who sought the dissolution of the dynastic holdings, found small comfort in Hungary, while Maria Theresa received there the first full commitment in her search for aid. This surprising turn resulted primarily from the happy convergence of political circumstances and her own quite remarkable abilities. From the first moment of her reign she had recognized that Hungarian support was essential and so she had quickly issued a confirmation of the Hungarian liberties. She had also wisely entrusted her interests to Count John Palffy, one of the leaders of the Hungarian nobility. Palffy understood that if Hungary were to have a place in Europe, if she were to fulfill her mission not only as the frontier of civilization but as a bridge between east and west, she must remain in community with the dynasty.

Maria Theresa's expression of trust in Palffy and in Hungary stimulated the Hungarians to immediate protestations of loyalty to the dynasty. Well aware of the symbolic importance of the crown of St. Stephen, Maria Theresa summoned the diet to prepare for the coronation. As early as January 26, 1741, Palffy had called to the *comitates* of Hungary for material aid. Within a month he was able to report specific pledges of men and horses to his sovereign. This response made a profound impression on the advisers of Maria Theresa, many of whom had warned her of the great danger of calling the turbulent Hungarians to arms. They would have much preferred that the Magyars send money rather than armed men. To be sure, the Hungarians were not vowing to take arms on the basis of some chivalric notion of one's obligation to fair princesses. There was political logic to their willingness, logic premised on specific guarantees of their liberties and privileges.

The coronation was a magnificent spectacle, containing all the ingredients of grand pageantry and romantic drama, but both before and after that memorable event much discussion and hard bargaining was required. One of the principal difficulties concerned Maria Theresa's desire to have Francis made co-regent with her and to have him regent-designate for any interregnum should she die before her heir came of age. Maria Theresa hoped to acquire this position for her husband in all her lands, for she believed this to be a necessary step in pressing his candidacy for the imperium. She had no intention of deferring real power to him, but such a position would have given him a nominal power base superior to that provided by Tuscany, and one which was at least partially "German." The Hungarians, however, were manifestly unwilling to give him that honor. Thus, when Maria Theresa arrived in Pressburg for the coronation on June 19, 1741, she was greeted by the traditional formula *Vivat Domina, et Rex Noster,* "Long Live our Mistress and King."

Her coronation oath contained new guarantees of the freedoms and privileges of the Hungarians as well as reiterating the conditions attendant to the Hungarian approval of the Pragmatic Sanction. Hungarian consent to the Sanction had stipulated that whoever inherited the other dynastic lands would be accepted as ruler of Hungary if the individual were a direct descendant of the Carlian, Josephian, or Leopoldine line of archduchesses. Should the succession within these limits fail, Hungary would receive anew the right to elect her own king. While in practice this limitation would be meaningless, since the likelihood of the Habsburg line dissipating so completely was not great, the unique status of Hungary had received another precedent. By her oath in 1741, Maria Theresa gave additional legal sanction to the dualism between Hungary and "non-Hungary" that would characterize the Habsburg state until its collapse. Parenthetically it might be noted that Maria Theresa would imbue the dualism with political reality because her subsequent reforms aimed at centralizing the government were basically limited to "non-Hungary."

For the moment, however, the important thing was that Maria Theresa had been duly crowned and had received a pledge of allegiance from the Hungarians. She still faced the problem of converting ceremonial acceptance and all the protestations of good will into the actuality of men and money with which she could protect her lands. The Estates had still to debate and decide a whole series of practical questions. Palffy's election as

Palatine of Hungary marked a hopeful beginning, but further agreements came hard and on several occasions the Estates seemed on the verge of dissolving. Underlying all the vexing questions which confronted those present was a persistent tension between Magyar and German. Throughout the summer the Diet discussed and did not act. The Estates rejected a renewed plea for a co-regency, quarreled about what to pledge as a coronation gift, and demanded that only men Hungarian-born be permitted in certain positions. The warnings of Maria Theresa's advisers were being substantiated: the Hungarians could not be trusted.

The allied drive into Austria had stalled at Linz as a result of Charles Albert of Bavaria's fear that Habsburg forces in Italy might invade his lands, and Frederick of Prussia continued to imply his willingness to make a separate truce with Maria Theresa. The tenuous character of the coalition arrayed against her must have comforted the young queen, but still she needed aid and allies, for no diplomatic arrangement could remove the ultimate threat of extinction. Only military victory could do that. Thus threatened, Maria Theresa on September 11, 1741, called the Chambers of the Hungarian Estates together and declared:

The disastrous situation of our affairs has moved us to lay before our dear and faithful states of Hungary the recent invasion of Austria, the danger now impending over this kingdom, and a proposal for the consideration of a remedy. The very existence of the kingdom of Hungary, of our own person, of our children, and our crown, are now at stake. Forsaken by all, we place our sole resource in the fidelity, arms and long-tried valour of the Hungarians; exhorting you, the states and orders, to deliberate without delay in this extreme danger, on the most effectual measures for the security of our person, of our children, and of our crown, and to carry them into immediate execution. In regard to ourself, the faithful states and orders of Hungary shall experience our hearty cooperation in all things, which may promote the pristine happiness of this ancient kingdom, and the honour of the people.[10]

In effect Maria Theresa proposed to arm the people of Hungary so that they might defend themselves against any possible attack. In response the Hungarian Estates moved to meet both of her most urgent requests. On September 20, they expressed their willingness to accept Francis as co-regent, albeit under conditions that made the honor only titular. Shortly thereafter they reasserted the promise to provide substantial military aid. The high drama of this moment has often obscured the real character of the event. Certainly there was a fierceness in the young queen's manner, rooted in the passionate conviction that she was in the right. The intensity of that conviction had led her to throw off the pessimistic counsels of most of her advisers, to press the battle, and to speak so directly to the proud and independent Hungarians. But she was both a consummate actress and a talented politician. She knew what was required to move the Hungarians to action and she sensed how she must approach them. Thus she offered them not a cowering princess to protect nor a haughty German monarch to obey, but a royal partner in the defense of mutual rights and privileges. Certainly her beauty touched the Hungarian nobles and her trust both flattered and honored them, but above all she convinced them that the preservation of the monarchy was in their best interest.[11] This she accomplished not only by her public appeal but by the hard bargaining carried on through Palffy and others. Maria Theresa had clearly demonstrated that she would rule as well as reign and in so doing had rallied her dominions. The real job of defense could now begin.

Maria Theresa's greatest strength lay in the disunity of her enemies. Efforts to divide the opposition had momentarily succeeded when Frederick signed an informal truce, the Protocol of Klein Schnellendorf (October 9, 1741). As a result, at the very moment when the Elector of Bavaria became Holy Roman Emperor (February 12, 1742), Habsburg armies were invading Bavaria; while Charles VII received his crown at Frankfurt, Austrian troops were in the streets of Munich. The hollowness of the crown was thus made manifest, for without a sufficient power base, the imperium was meaningless. Even in Paris, Charles was known derisively as "John Lackland." The flood tide that had threatened to engulf Austria was ebbing.

Already on February 1, Austria's position on still another front had vastly improved with the signing of the Convention of Turin with Carlo Emanuele of Sardinia. In Italy the Austrian position had been threatened by the unabated ambitions of Elizabeth Farnese and Bourbon Spain. Seizing upon the embarrassment of the Habsburgs in the north, Elizabeth Farnese saw an opportunity to gain patrimonies in Italy for her sons. The natural choice of ally for the Habsburgs in Italy was Sardinia, for its king, Carlo Emanuele, could not be expected to support an extension of Bourbon influence in the peninsula. On the other hand, he was loath to ally himself with a power so sorely threatened as Austria. He hoped to play both sides to Sardinia's advantage, but when Spain increased her troop concentration in Italy, the issue was settled in favor of an alliance with Austria.

In the north a new crisis was coming, a crisis generated by Austria's very success. Frederick could not stand idly by while Austria reestablished her power, for Maria Theresa had not resigned herself to the loss of Silesia. Frederick had already openly expressed the tentative nature of his agreement to a truce; and thus his decision to reenter the war in force was not surprising. In his renewed offensive, however, Frederick did not act in close alliance with France, for he wished to avoid entanglements from which he might find it difficult to disengage himself. His purpose in reentering the war had little to do with any feeling of obligation to the original alliance; rather, it was derived from a desire to reaffirm the gains he had made by his first offensive. He would later console the French leader Belle-Isle: "I look upon this affair as a navigation undertaken by several with one same object, but which, being upset by a shipwreck, places each of the navigators under the necessity of saving himself by swimming, and landing wherever he can."[12] Though angered by Prussia's renewed attack, Maria Theresa recognized that Austria could not fight both France and Prussia simultaneously nor could she fight either without extensive English support. Thus, she gave way to continued English pressure to arrange a peace with Frederick. The English, who had no interest in a war with Prussia and who interpreted the whole struggle as a conflict with Bourbon ambitions for European hegemony, gained the leverage they needed to bring their ally into line by the Prussian victory at Chotusitz (May 17, 1742), a sad baptismal gift for Maria Theresa's fifth child, Maria Christina, born May 13, 1742.

The Prussian victory forced Maria Theresa to make peace with Frederick, but on both sides the rivalry intensified and became increasingly personal. The Treaty of Breslau (July 28, 1742) reconfirmed and extended the earlier Protocol of Klein Schnellendorf. The benefits of peace with Prussia were quickly apparent as Austria mounted a successful campaign against Prague in the process transforming the war from a struggle over succession to a balance-of-power conflict. The crowning of Maria Theresa in Prague (May 11, 1743) symbolized the transform- ation: the Habsburg lands would pass to the heiress in accord- ance with the Pragmatic Sanction. But even as she received the crown she remembered that the dominions had not devolved to her undivided, for Silesia had been lost, and the hope of regaining it persisted.

In that hope there flickered the consciousness of the new political reality that in the years ahead would reshape European diplomatic relations. Maria Theresa was among the first European leaders to understand that the traditional rivalries and alliances had lost their meaning. At this point her awareness was tentative and would grow to conviction only with time and subsequent events, but the particularity of her antagonism toward Frederick henceforth entered all her calculations. Maria Theresa thus did little to ease Frederick's mounting concern that Austrian victories were but a prelude to an attempted reconquest of Silesia. The allied victory at Dettingen (June 27, 1743) and the closing of an alliance among Austria, England, and Sardinia, the Treaty of Worms (September 13, 1743), which promised to free Maria Theresa to turn her attention to Germany, led directly to Fred- erick's decision to reenter the war in the summer of 1744. The renewed threat to Bohemia had disastrous effects upon Austria's war effort elsewhere, especially in the Lowlands, but Maria Theresa responded to the threat with almost gleeful indignation. The Second Silesian War intensified her belief that only the restoration of Silesia could compensate for her monarchy's travail and that Frederick of Prussia was her most dangerous foe.

The German front assumed further importance with the sudden death of Charles VII on January 20, 1745. Confronted by a new opportunity to acquire the imperium for her husband and her dynasty, Maria Theresa sought to guarantee the election by clearing Germany of all French troops. To that end the dissolu- tion of the Franco-Bavarian alliance, the *raison d'être* of the French presence in Germany, contributed greatly. For the French the natural candidate for the imperium was Maximilian Joseph, the seventeen-year-old son of Charles VII, but the young prince had no wish to be a puppet of the French. Throwing aside the tutelage of his French minister, Chevigny, Maximilian opened negotiations with Maria Theresa that resulted in the Treaty of Füssen (May 2, 1745). By this treaty the young elector received back his dynastic lands conquered by Austria and in return he guaranteed the Pragmatic Sanction and placed his electoral vote at the queen's disposal.

In Germany, aside from Maximilian, the only alternative to the Archduke Francis was Augustus III, Elector of Saxony and King of Poland. Unlike Maximilian, Augustus would willingly have offered himself as a candidate, but, on the one hand, Frederick II was not particularly happy with the idea and, on the other hand, Augustus felt too closely bound to the interests of the Habsburgs at that point. Indeed, by an agreement signed just twelve days before Charles' sudden death, January 8, 1745, Saxony had promised to support Maria Theresa against Prussia. However eager he was for the imperium, Augustus wanted land more than the title, and the relationship with Austria seemed more promising in that regard.

No rival candidate was forthcoming; even the victory of the Prussians over the Austrians and Saxons at Hohenfriedberg (June 4, 1745) could not alter that fact. Determined not to allow a repetition of 1742, Maria Theresa had ordered her armies to move toward Frankfurt, thus guaranteeing a "friendly" atmosphere during the election. While the Saxon elector continued to play coy with the French, the presence of the Habsburg army under Traun militated against the reassertion of French influence on the election. Despite the encouragement of the electors of Brandenburg and the Palatinate, the French did not attempt to alter the military situation along the Main, for to have done so would have required a weakening of their position in the Low Countries, to which they had now decided to devote their attention. Consequently, on September 13, 1745, Francis was elected Holy Roman Emperor.

Maria Theresa had already planned her journey to Frankfurt, combining practical politics with connubial pride. While desirous of seeing her husband enjoy his accession to so signal a dignity, Maria Theresa also recognized the benefits of showing herself before the German peoples. The enthusiastic greeting she received at Heidelberg despite the opposition of the Elector-Palatine demonstrates that she assessed the situation correctly. But she rebuffed suggestions that she should be crowned empress with her husband, pleading the state of her health, being once again pregnant. More likely, however, she declined the honor because of her wifely concern that the day should belong entirely to Francis. Even so, for those who witnessed the coronation, the clearest memory was of the beautiful young wife and mother.[13] On her entrance into the city there was rejoicing. While she viewed the procession from a balcony overlooking the route, many eyes focused on her and responded to her cheers and clappings rather than to the pomp and ceremony. The enthusiasm of the crowd reached its peak when Maria Theresa waved her handkerchief to her emperor-husband and shouted "Vivat."

Such moments when she could be a private person and feel a joy for her loved ones alone were increasingly rare. In part as a result of that deprivation the intensity of her passion for Francis seemed to sharpen. There was a devouring possessiveness about her affirmations of love. Francis never returned to his Tuscan domain after the brief sojourn of 1739 because Maria Theresa could not tolerate even a brief separation from him. In 1744 when he expressed a desire to resume a military career she demurred. As she described it to her sister, the Archduchess Maria Anna,

> I was sick with anger and chagrin and made the old one [Francis] ill with my wickedness. . . . At first I only made light of the idea, but finally I saw that he was serious. I resorted to our usual instruments, caresses and tears, as much as one can do with a husband of nine years, but I got nowhere although he is the best husband in the world. I finally resumed my anger which served only to make both of us ill . . . I gave up fighting him, but shilly-shallied from day to day to win time, but if he does go I shall either follow him or shut myself in a convent.[14]

Maria Theresa had her way, although she did permit him to participate in the campaign of 1745 meant to protect the electors at Frankfurt from French pressure. That concession on her part seemed a necessary sacrifice: Francis needed to do something to win his crown. She remained, however, intensely jealous of his time.

Not without aptitude, as his financial dealings make abundantly clear (he was largely responsible for developing an enormous family fortune), Francis nonetheless lacked the courage and endurance to serve effectively as a co-regent, even had Maria Theresa been disposed to share real power.[15] Clearly she had decided not to do so at the very beginning of her reign; an unusually perceptive judge of men, even of those whom she

loved, but also inclined to hasty judgment, she had early concluded that her adored "old one" could not bear the responsibilities of power. Physically, however, he served her well.

In all things she was passionate. The demands of state meant
that in the moments of pleasure she could hoard there was a
striking intensity. She laughed abundantly and during the carni-
vals she danced with boundless energy. Much of her appeal to
the Viennese was that she so obviously could enjoy life. Her
tomb in the basement of the Capuchin Church, the construction
of which began as early as 1741, provides a peculiarly baroque
commentary: the sculptor has transformed the tomb into a lovers'
couch, with the imperial couple, portrayed in the prime of life,
reclining gracefully, yet gazing intently into one another's eyes.
During their marriage, which was an essential anchor in her
life, she bore Francis sixteen children, all fruits of her love for
him. During the War of the Austrian Succession itself she deliv-
ered seven children—in addition to Joseph and Maria Christina
mentioned before, they were Maria Elizabeth (August 23, 1743),
Karl Joseph (February 1, 1745), Maria Amalia (February 26,
1746), Peter Leopold (May 15, 1747) and Maria Caroline (September 18, 1748). Childbearing seemed a natural part of her
life and hardly interfered with the tasks of state. Usually, after
initial discomfort, she thrived on pregnancy, and despite the
frantic warnings of her doctors had no time for long confine-
ments. The tides of war might fluctuate, but Maria Theresa with
constancy fulfilled her role as a producer of children. Her enemy,
the misogynist Frederick, thought it singularly vulgar.

Unlike many of her contemporaries, Maria Theresa had a
passion for fidelity as well. There were rumors that Maria Theresa
had an affair with Count Anton Grassalkovich during her visit to
Hungary in 1741, but no clear evidence to substantiate them
exists.[16] Indeed, Otto von Podewils, Prussia's foreign minister,
whose diplomatic reports provide a significant source for this
period and who would have been pleased to uncover any scandal
tarnishing the image of his master's enemy, almost ruefully
described Maria Theresa's moral conduct as bourgeois. Had she
known this Maria Theresa would have laughed for having disappointed the Prussian wolf.

Maria Theresa's growing preoccupation with Frederick had
two corollaries: disillusionment with England and dissipation of
the sense of threat from France. Both proceeded apace. In 1743,

despite early English reluctance to enter the war and Great Britain's role in producing the Breslau settlement, the traditional system in Europe seemed intact. Maria Theresa had vigorously rejected French overtures for a settlement in Bohemia and a change in English leadership promised a more vigorous involvement in the war. The Italian campaigns of 1743-1744, however, provided a brutal awakening for Maria Theresa.

In whatever strategy Austria might adopt in Italy, the English alliance, which provided a subsidy and the support of the Mediterranean fleet, was vital. English interests, however, diverged from Austrian interests. While Maria Theresa wished to drive the Bourbons from the peninsula, the English wished to prevent any power from establishing hegemony there, to establish a power balance in which they could act as ultimate arbiter.[17] To that end Great Britain supported Sardinia and Maria Theresa found herself forced to make an alliance with Carlo Emanuele (Treaty of Worms) on his terms.

Increasingly obvious also was England's determination not to make any settlement inimical to Prussia.[18] Maria Theresa desired recompense for the loss of Silesia; specifically she sought to acquire German lands. The Marchese d'Ormea, Carlo Emanuele's chief minister, first proposed that this might be accomplished by trading Habsburg lands in Italy for Bavaria. The proposal had appeal for both Sardinia and Austria: for the former it meant replacing the Habsburgs in Italy by a lesser Germany dynasty and for the latter it meant creating a contiguous power base in Germany as well as removing the chief rival to the imperial title. Maria Theresa had only limited enthusiasm for the exchange, preferring the restoration of Silesia itself. Secondarily, she hesitated to deal lightly with the one land where her husband was lord. But she was willing to discuss it; English opposition sidetracked the project. The English feared the strengthening of the Habsburg position in Germany would provoke new hostilities between Prussia and Austria, which in turn would weaken Austria's commitment to the war with France.[19]

Following the Treaty of Worms the French had decided to increase their own military commitment and to direct it primarily at England. Consequently, the Netherlands became the principal stage of the war. Frederick's reentry into the war confirmed French strategy, for with Austrian forces preoccupied with the defense of Bohemia they could not put pressure on the Rhine front. Indeed, Maria Theresa hoped that England and Holland would carry the greatest burden of defense in the Low Countries. She certainly did not mean to concede Habsburg lands there without a struggle if for no other reason than that her beloved sister Maria Anna and twice brother-in-law Charles of Lorraine were vice-regents there, but Maria Theresa had already evolved a clear set of priorities. Given the limited resources of the monarchy, the immediate struggle with Prussia had first call, then the Italian war, and only then the Netherlands. Pressured by the English to increase her military force there, Maria Theresa consciously and specifically chose not to divert her energies from Germany.

The allied campaign of 1744 in the Netherlands failed abysmally and in 1745 the war had continued to go badly. Almost simultaneously with the coronation of Francis (October 4), the queen received word that Austrian forces under Charles of Lorraine had suffered a crushing defeat at Soor (September 30). The English once again exerted pressure on Vienna to come to terms with Prussia. Such a prospect was repugnant to Maria Theresa. Although she recognized that Austria could not continue the war against both France and Prussia, she responded to English suggestions by querying, "Why are there less hopes of detaching France than Prussia?"[20] She anticipated that one more campaign against Prussia might bring success. As a result, she pressed the war; at the same time, she made overtures to the French.

As early as mid-1743, Maria Theresa, angered by the behavior of the English in the Italian crisis, had expressed a willingness to establish closer relations with the French. By mid-1745, Maria Theresa had received still further and clearer proof that the long-standing alliance with the maritime powers was not fulfilling its expected function. Only the persistent opposition of her husband and his brother, neither yet reconciled to the final loss of Lorraine, had discouraged her, but Frederick's treachery in 1744 overcame this objection. As long as France was regarded as the chief foe of the dynasty, then whatever its inadequacies the alliance with the maritime powers was essential. But if France were not the archenemy, if instead Prussia were to be considered as the primary foe, the apparent affinity between Britain and Prussia rendered that alliance impotent in dealing with the real needs of Austria. By 1745, Maria Theresa, at least, had made this shift.

The French themselves had made inquiries through the Austrian representative in Switzerland as early as September, 1744. Again in early 1745 discussions were opened. In these preliminary meetings the French talked always in terms of allowing Frederick to retain Silesia, not because they particularly liked Frederick, but because they did not want Austria to be too strong. To Maria Theresa this was clearly unsatisfactory, for the whole purpose of negotiations with France was to give her a free hand in dealing with Prussia. Even so, the alliance with England was equally restrictive, indeed perhaps more so, since further discussions with France might lead to a compromise, while the English support of Frederick was not negotiable. (On August 26, 1745, England had concluded the convention of Hanover with Frederick by which Prussia's possession of Silesia, as stated in the Treaty of Breslau, was guaranteed.) Bartenstein, who had become one of her chief advisers despite her initial reservations about him, also encouraged Maria Theresa. As a result, in late November, 1745, she commissioned Count Friedrich Harrach with full powers to negotiate a settlement with France.

Harrach's discussions with Vaulgrenant, the French representative in Dresden, quickly revealed, however, that the French were unwilling to retreat from their position that Frederick should retain Silesia. Therefore Harrach was instructed to open talks with Prussia on the basis of the Convention of Hanover. To the very last moment Maria Theresa was willing to negotiate with the French, but Harrach, despite his own dislike for Prussia, judged France to be irreconcilable. As a result, on December 25, 1745, he signed the Treaty of Dresden with the Prussian ambassador, Otto von Podewils. Essentially, the treaty reiterated the earlier settlements. Frederick's control of Silesia was confirmed, in return for which he validated the election of Francis. In retrospect, the first loss of Silesia (1741) was final. For all her hopes and plans Maria Theresa never regained effective control of the lost province, but in 1745 it would yet be a long time, almost two decades, before she could resign herself to that loss. The Treaty of Dresden was a strategic necessity, not a final concession. To Maria Theresa a simple fact explained the strategic necessity: Austria's virtual dependence on England.

Given the weaknesses of her own dominions, their disorganization and paucity of revenue, that dependency was unavoidable, but her sensitivity to it eventually culminated in a broad reappraisal of Habsburg foreign policy and intensified Maria Theresa's desire for substantial internal reforms. Peace with Prussia was required in order that a future war with Prussia could be waged—and won. With Prussia withdrawn from the conflict, Maria Theresa's goal was not the defeat of France, but a reasonable peace, one that would allow her to reform and rebuild the inheritance she had so tenaciously defended.

In Italy, Austria's position began to improve during 1746. Choosing now between Italy and the Netherlands, Maria Theresa unhesitatingly preferred the former. In the Low Countries French successes accelerated, culminating with the capitulation of Brussels (February 21, 1746) which, for all intents and purposes ended the war. Subsequent hostilities were merely desultory maneuverings for position while the real action proceeded at the conference table.

The Dutch, with English approval, had opened negotiations with France even before the fall of Brussels. The French, still operating on the premise that the Habsburgs were their natural and irreconcilable enemies, assumed the discussions would lead to a separate peace between France and the maritime powers, but England now pressed for the participation of Austria and Sardinia. From September, 1746, to May, 1747, the belligerents conferred at Breda without marked progress. Negotiations were transferred to Aix-la-Chapelle and then suspended as the battle was wearily rejoined in the summer of 1747. But France was exhausted and England satisfied that she had achieved her major aims. Peace then seemed inevitable and Maria Theresa had to make the most of it.

To that end, when the conference at Aix-la-Chapelle reopened, Maria Theresa dispatched Wenzel Anton von Kaunitz-Rittberg to represent her.[21] Maria Theresa approached the talks with almost no faith in the English. To Kaunitz she observed, "It is depressing to find oneself in such circumstances and even more depressing to know less harm can be expected from the enemy than from the allies."[22] To avoid being forced into making undesirable concessions by her allies, Maria Theresa instructed Kaunitz to treat directly with the French and Spanish. Thus, as soon as the French representative, Saint-Severin, arrived,

Kaunitz opened discussions with him. In such discussions, however, Austria was at a distinct disadvantage, for if the purpose of separate talks was to avoid making concessions, then Austria had nothing in particular to offer the French, who were well aware that only agreement with England could produce a general peace. But Maria Theresa's determination to outmaneuver her allies, and the initial friendliness of Saint-Severin seemed to bode well for Kaunitz's mission. The French, however, were only dividing the alliance that they might profit, and on April 30 they signed a preliminary agreement with the English and the Dutch. All other interested powers were invited to countersign the agreement, though simultaneously the original signatory powers added a secret article by which they agreed that any power refusing to accede to the treaty would be excluded from the advantages of the agreement.

Rather than condemning the duplicity of the French, Maria Theresa blamed the English for this setback. She instructed Kaunitz to continue negotiations with the French, and to sign the agreement. The latter she saw as only a preliminary accord, and one therefore whose worst features might yet be corrected. Hope for such correction could come only from the French, not from the English, for she was certain the French would recognize the need to obtain her good will. For Austria, the approbation of the maritime powers was no longer the essential aim; the neutrality of the French in the Austro-Prussian conflict was now primary.

Following the official approval of the preliminary agreement (May 23), Kaunitz tried to delay the signing of a definitive treaty, at the same time continuing talks with the French. The crucial point in these discussions was to obtain a promise that the French would not guarantee the Treaty of Dresden. The French were quick to offer any assistance to bar Prussian pretentions to the imperium in the future, but their need for peace discouraged them from going further. Thus again the discussions were fruitless and, on October 18, the French, English, and Dutch signed the Treaty of Aix-la-Chapelle. While certain concessions had been made to Austria in the Low Countries and an article asserting the sovereignty of Maria Theresa was included, Austria refused to be a contracting party to the treaty, though promising approval. This maneuver was largely an act of protest. Maria Theresa's disappointment over proceedings at Aix-la-Chapelle were further darkened by the death at birth of her tenth child Maria Caroline (September 18, 1748).

Despite the loss of Silesia and the failure to gain compensation, Maria Theresa could not regard the war as wasted effort. The principle of the indivisibility of the dynastic lands had been defended and the dynasty itself preserved; indeed, its future seemed secured by the burgeoning family circle. For the latter Francis too must receive some credit, but for the former Maria Theresa bore full responsibility. Short of determining actual battlefield strategy Maria Theresa had directed the war effort and the concomitant diplomacy, setting the priorities and rendering the crucial decisions. She proceeded, not without error, but with a firmness born of youthful vigor, confident conviction, native guile, and a certain innocence which, however, by 1748 she had lost.

CHAPTER III

The Apprentice Monarch

FIERCELY, YET REVERENTLY, MARIA THERESA HAD ASSUMED HER role, convinced that since God had so ordered her life she must fulfill her duty and seek the best interests of her lands. In the midst of war those interests were mere survival, but she well knew that more was required. In retrospect she stated:

... After the Peace of Dresden my one endeavor was to inform myself of the situation and resources of each Province, and then to acquire a thorough understanding and picture of the abuses which had crept into them and their administrative services, resulting in the utmost confusion and distressfulness.[1]

To understand the sequel one must have some knowledge of what she discovered.

Maria Theresa inherited a monarchy which in its essential form derived from the reign of Ferdinand II (1619-1638), particularly the policies pursued after the Battle of White Mountain (1620): the monarchy had triumphed over the estates, yet the culmination of this victory, an integral absolute state in lieu of a *Ständestaat* was still unrealized. Ferdinand had not attempted to eliminate the estates after he had subordinated them because the conflict with them centered on confessional, not military or fiscal, questions. Their survival perpetuated the dualism between estates and central control. In asserting the unity of the dynastic lands, however, the Pragmatic Sanction had prepared the way for the emergence of state power.[2]

The principal weakness of the monarchy was the excessive particularism of the provincial nobility. In the seventeenth century the Habsburgs had overcome the separatist tendencies of the estates, but they had not rooted out the cause of this tendency, the existence of particularistic rights and privileges among the local nobility. Indeed, they strengthened this element by seeking to tie the nobility more closely to the monarchy through the granting of places in the provincial administration. Ferdinand III (1637-1658) and Leopold I (1658-1705) created a specifically Austrian social class by transferring Bohemian and even Hungarian lands to German nobles while encouraging the nobility in general to enter the administration. They granted more diplomas of imperial nobility than had been issued in any comparable period, and permitted the establishment of a majority of the entails, including those of the older families.

By the 1740's this pattern had taken root and the administration was in the hands of a nobility firmly based in the Habsburg dominions. Thus, a figure like Johann Christoph Bartenstein (1689-1767), a Thuringian Protestant who entered Austrian service and was converted to Roman Catholicism, while a familiar type in the seventeenth century, was an exception in the eighteenth. Now typical were men like Sinzendorf, who descended from a Tyrolean knightly family that had been reconverted to Roman Catholicism in the 1600's; and Kaunitz, the descendant of an ancient Bohemian family which had dedicated itself to state service in the years after White Mountain. This aristocratic service group enhanced its position by its assertion of cultural as well as political leadership. Acquiring its education at foreign universities and through travel, the nobility supported, if it did not actually participate in, cultural activity, thus promoting an esteem which other German aristocracies lacked.[3]

An independent aristocracy persisted, but its situation can best be described by reference to the two branches of the Kaunitz family. These two lines were descended from Ulrich V, who in the civil and religious strife of the sixteenth century had been one of the chief foes of the Roman Catholic party. This conviction produced a loss of wealth and a threat to freedom and life as well. Ulrich's eldest sons, Charles' and Frederick, had strongly supported his views. Frederick's descendants (the Bohemian line) retained the baronial title, but were content to live a steadfast and unbrilliant existence in Bohemia. The Moravian line, descending from Leo Wilhelm, a younger son of Ulrich's second marriage who had not been involved in the struggle, dedicated itself to service of the state. As a result, in 1642 Leo Wilhelm was made a count of Bohemia; in 1682, his son Dominic Andreas was elevated to count of the empire; and finally, in 1764, the dynasty's greatest son, Wenzel Anton, was made prince.[4]

The continuance of an independent aristocracy, or at least one not participating in state service, underlined the fact that the social structure remained basically seignorial since the most important unifying force was manorial control of peasants, villages, markets, and towns. No burgher class rose to challenge the importance of this control. Austria was not a land of towns, but of one city and the countryside. Nor was Vienna a Paris, for the burghers as they became wealthy tended to withdraw to the country where they might establish their respectability through land holding, while the nobles, though drawn into the administration, continued their ties with the land, since the basic units of the government were still the *Länder*.

In her analysis of the weaknesses of the monarchy at the time of her accession, Maria Theresa criticized most sharply the administrative structure, particularly the retention of forms which subordinated the common interests of the dynastic lands to local interests. The alienation of control to local estates and administrators meant that these particular and selfish interests were being served first. Furthermore, the occupancy of governmental positions was no longer regarded as a privilege but as a right, indeed even as a right of specific noble families. Thus the monarch was deprived of any means of remedying particular problems. A dangerous ramification of provincial particularism was the disunity and selfish concerns of the ministers and advisers of the monarch, and the unwillingness of these men to commit themselves on difficult questions, for they were protecting both their high status in the monarchy and their local power. If, in such circumstances, a ruler were indecisive, he could hardly be otherwise, for a king is not infallible, and lacking advice he must vacillate. In saying this Maria Theresa emphasized that on her accession she lacked counsel as well as resources—she may also have provided herself with a rationalization for her father's characteristic indecision.

In brief, the structure of the central administration at her accession was as follows: the chief advisory councils were the Privy Conference, the Financial Conference, and a committee which acted as the advisory board for financial problems related to the military.[5] The arbitrary and ill-defined spheres of activity made any unity on this level impossible. There were four chancelleries (the Austrian chancellery which administered not only a portion of the dynastic lands, but also supervised foreign trade; and chancelleries for Bohemia, Hungary, and Transylvania) and they were usually in conflict with one another. It was through the chancelleries that the disruptive influence of the estates was most frequently expressed. In addition to the chancelleries there was an office for the Italian and Netherlands provinces. The finance administration was divided into three parts, and again the jurisdictional lines were inadequately drawn. The Exchequer was in effect the central office, but the existence of a separate banking committee made coordination of fiscal policy and credit policy difficult. Adding to the confusion was still another agency which became a kind of central counting house. The various financial prerogatives which the War Council possessed further disordered financial matters. In turn, the lack of coordination between it and the Exchequer weakened the ability of the War Council to function.

Quite early in the war it was apparent that a basic reform of the monarchy was required, a reform far broader than a mere administrative reorganization. It was equally clear that so fundamental a revision could not be carried out during the war. Austria must survive before she could rebuild, but survival itself required reform. The reforms conceived and carried out before 1749 had as their aim the deliverance of the monarchy from the immediate threat of destruction. They were tentative and yet specific, most of them relating directly to the conduct of the war. In retrospect they reflect the first traces of the political personality and principles of the fairest of the Habsburgs.

The first major alteration of the military administration came in 1743-1744, when Maria Theresa dissolved the separate offices for Austrian and non-Austrian lands within the War Council, thus rejecting the idea that the military needs of any one part of her domain were independent of the military needs of the whole. This was followed in 1745 by the expansion of the powers of the president of the War Council, and simultaneously by the queen's increased involvement in the deliberations and decisions of the Council. In 1746, the military reform was extended by a reorganization of the General War Commissariat. Raised to the level of a direct court office, the Commissariat was empowered not only with military police functions, but also with the surveillance of all logistical problems. Despite the opposition of the Exchequer, which saw this maneuver as an alienation of its jurisdiction, the Commissariat henceforth functioned as an autonomous bureau with carefully described functions. Though only partial and blunted by bureaucratic resistance to change, these reforms significantly improved the governance of the Austrian army by the end of the war and created the framework for a more effective military force in the future.

The corollary of military reorganization was financial reform, for an army without money cannot function. Here Maria Theresa confronted far graver problems. The treasury was almost empty, Charles VI having depleted it by granting extensive subsidies to others in an effort to confirm the Pragmatic Sanction. The state debt had increased almost seventy percent in Charles' reign, and attempts to increase royal revenues in that time had succeeded only in creating more tension between the estates and the central government. The loss of Silesia, a major source of revenue (in 1739, Silesia had contributed twenty-five percent, two million gulden, of the direct tax revenue collected from the hereditary lands), had compounded the financial problem. Given the severity of the problem, the measures adopted to solve it also had to be severe. In 1741 Maria Theresa dissolved the Finance Conference and invested Count Starhemberg, for thirty-five years the director of the Vienna City Bank, with the advisory function it formerly held. To further centralize financial control in the Exchequer and to reduce administrative costs she subsequently (1745) eliminated the central counting house. The reforms were not a matter of simple amalgamation, but involved the separation and delimitation of certain functions: thus the separation of minting and mining concerns from those of commerce. Almost all the reforms attempted at this time shared one feature in common: they were ultimately centralizing reforms, for they involved the extension and definition of the authority of the central administration as opposed to the provincial authorities. In 1746, for example, Maria Theresa established a Universal Commercial Directorate which was immediately under her jurisdiction and which had as its primary function the coordination of commerce throughout the monarchy. However, the chancelleries retained control over the Directorate, thus obstructing any real uniformity in economic policy.

This flaw manifested the basic weakness of all the early reforms, and proved that a more fundamental change was required.

The flaw was not in the administration of the monarchy as such, but in its constitutional structure. The correction of this basic fault needed more tranquil times—and younger, more imaginative men than those who surrounded the young queen in the first years of her reign. As loyal as they had been, the older ministers inherited from her father were nevertheless products of the old system. Many of them retained the prejudices of estate particularism which would be the chief target of Theresian reform. Even in political administration Maria Theresa had etched the outline of some future critical changes. Thus when a jurisdictional dispute over newly acquired lands in the southeast (Banat, Slavonia, and parts of Transylvania) arose between the War Council and the Exchequer, Maria Theresa in 1745 created a commission directly responsible to her which would administer the lands. The War Council retained only military jurisdiction, and the Exchequer certain specific revenue controls. The move reflected the rationalization and centralization of jurisdiction that would characterize subsequent reforms.

The most decisive change which Maria Theresa effected at this time in the monarchy's political structure was the removal of foreign affairs and archducal affairs from the Austrian chancellery and the creation of a separate Court and State Chancellery. The decree of February 14, 1742, assumed that one function of the new Chancellery was the supervision of civil and criminal justice. In 1745 the Chancellery appealed to her for guidance in a particular matter. This appeal encouraged her to consider the feasibility of separating judicial and executive functions entirely. While no steps were taken to formalize this separation, a revolutionary concept in Austria, she did articulate the principle in dealing with the specific issue. In 1749 the creation of a separate judicial system enacted the principle. Significantly, Friedrich Wilhelm Count Haugwitz, the main author of the reforms of 1749, was already a trusted friend of the queen by 1745-1746. The reform embodied in the decree of 1742 was not fully realized, primarily because the first chancellor, Count Corfiz Ulfeld, concerned himself largely with court and dynastic matters, while foreign affairs remained the domain of the Privy Conference. Not until the appointment of Kaunitz to succeed Ulfeld in 1753 was the process completed. Even before then, however, Maria Theresa had eliminated the primacy of the Austrian chancellery and Kaunitz, like Haugwitz, had become a trusted servant of the queen.

The last piece of advice Maria Theresa set forth in her political testament was that "The most important obligation of a monarch is the selection of his advisers."[6] While of necessity relying upon the advisers of her father when she first came to power, she realized that one of her most critical tasks was to form a government of her own from men of her own choosing. One of her most significant achievements in the period 1740-1748 was the recruitment of those who would be her chief advisers and aides in the years ahead, men such as Haugwitz and Kaunitz. The character of these men emphasizes two important things about the monarch they both served: first her ability to recognize and to use talent however varied the wrapping, and second her intention to be advised not ruled by those around her. Apparently recognizing that she herself lacked an inventive mind, she sought to use the originality of others, but conscious too of her obligations as sovereign she would not allow any of her officials a totally free hand. When they pursued goals agreeable to her, however, she gave them unremitting support.

Historically Haugwitz seems a faceless man (perhaps a remarkable feat for an individual ill-favored physically), and there are no adequate biographical studies of him.[7] A Silesian and originally a Lutheran, he was converted to Roman Catholicism and worked his way up in the Silesian administration. Fleeing to Vienna after the Prussian invasion, he was named to govern the remnants of the Silesian province. Maria Theresa, struck by the incisive memoranda which he prepared, took note of his accomplishments in Silesia and came to see in him a crucial instrument for her future plans.

He was truly sent to me by Providence, for to break the deadlock I needed such a man, honorable, disinterested, without predispositions, and with neither ambition nor hangers-on, who supported what was good because he saw it to be good, of magnanimous disinterestedness and attachment to his monarch, with great capacity and industry and untiring diligence, not afraid to come into the open or to draw on himself the unjust hatred of interested parties.[8]

Awkward and unrefined, Haugwitz had few friends and so threw himself all the more enthusiastically into his labors. Less brilliant, less at ease at court—and less erratic and eccentric—

than Kaunitz, Haugwitz earned Maria Theresa's confidence by his "industry and untiring diligence" and so was able to introduce sweeping reforms. His failings as an administrator and as a political animal contributed to the eventual dilution of those reforms and the dissipation of his own authority, but to the end he remained a trusted and loyal friend of his monarch.

In contrast, Kaunitz seems eminently visible. Honest he doubtless was (though not above collecting subsidies from foreign governments); he too belonged to no cliques; but self-interest and bias were clearly evident in him for all his claims to dispassionate rationality. Vain, pompous, and arrogant, he minced across the stage of history with such a collection of personal eccentricities that it is difficult to understand how he even had the time to accomplish what he did, much less how Maria Theresa was able to tolerate him. A contemporary remarked that Kaunitz's character gave rise to reflections "on the contradictions of which human personalities consist and how one can combine the qualities of a superb mind with ridiculous traits which even defy extravagance."[9] Almost pathologically desirous of gaining the approval of his superiors, he fawned and wheedled and pouted, thus alienating many members of the court. Granted approval, he assumed the airs of a man whose every word and every idea pulsated with truth and whose sacred right it was to correct the mistakes of others, thus further antagonizing the courtiers. He possessed a certain charm, the result of his wit and broad cultural interests, but he reserved that charm for the royal family and for those from whom he had something to gain. Hardly pious, not eminently chaste, a hypochondriac, he seemed an unlikely favorite for Maria Theresa (and indeed they never were personally close), but, like Haugwitz, a warmer, humbler man, Kaunitz had an incisive mind and was more artful in seeking his ends, ends which he frequently shared with his monarch. Neither a *Realpolitiker* in the Bismarckian sense nor a genuine statesman of the Enlightenment (unless the Enlightenment was a charade), Kaunitz shared the political philosophy of Maria Theresa though he expressed it in rationalistic terms. It has been said that he could serve Joseph II because their means were similar, but that he always felt himself to be Maria Theresa's minister because their objectives were the same.

Of the advisers she inherited from her father only Bartenstein long continued to serve an important role.[10] At the time of her accession, Maria Theresa was not kindly disposed toward him, for she suspected him—she later admitted erroneously—of having urged her father to find a more suitable husband for her than Francis and of sponsoring the suggestion that she be passed over in favor of her sister during the grim days of 1739. (Robinson had long before remarked "that there is no more probability of her forgetting the very individual government, and the very individual husband which she thinks herself born to, than of her forgiving the authors of her losing either.")[11] Yet subsequently she credited him with having saved the monarchy in the first years of her reign. Sensitive of his social inferiority, yet keenly aware of his talents and jealous of the honors those talents had achieved, Bartenstein was not an attractive personality, but he was incorruptible and was sincerely attached to the interests of his adopted government. He served a crucial role in the first decades of Maria Theresa's rule, if for no other reason than that he was always willing to assert his views, which though not infallible were at least founded on genuine conviction. (His conversion to Roman Catholicism, which opened his way to advancement in Habsburg service, was not based on mere opportunism. He was converted only after careful soul-searching, and when he was convinced of the truth of Catholic teaching as he understood it.) This "prickly man, precise and pedantic to a fault" would remain among her most influential advisers for fifteen years.

Haugwitz and Kaunitz were but two of the new men who in the future would serve Maria Theresa so well and who already by 1748 had begun to move in orbit around her. They were a motley collection—cantankerous, assertive, individualistic, indeed a collection, not a group. Maria Theresa chose them not for their charm or their social graces, but for their political or administrative talents. The one thing they had in common was devotion to the empress-queen. Maria Theresa was very much a man's woman. Though she had feminine acquaintances she had few close friends of her own sex and no advisers. Her sister Maria Anna came closest to being a genuine confidant.[12] Until her marriage in 1744 to Francis' brother Charles and her subsequent departure to the Netherlands to serve as Maria Theresa's vice-regent in Brussels, Maria Anna lived at the Hofburg. The sisters were quite close, intriguing together to accomplish the second Lorraine marriage even over the opposition of their mother. The letters they exchanged in 1744 reveal the strength of their bond, and Maria Anna's all too brief tenure as vice-regent demonstrated qualities not inferior to Maria Theresa's. The older sister glowed with pride on hearing that the younger refused to flee from her capital as the French armies approached. Tragically, however, following a pregnancy that ended in a still-birth, Maria Anna sickened and died. In her grief Maria Theresa wrote Gerhard Van Swieten, who had attended her sister:

> The most overwhelming blow which the Gracious Lord could deliver to me is the loss of my sister. The tenderness with which I have viewed her increased every day, and time which should heal such wounds will only increase it the more. My health has sustained this blow as it has many others and although in my ninth month [she then carried her eighth child Maria Amalia] I conduct myself as required. I see clearly God's wishes operating in me, supporting me with his gracious favor to accept the travail, the sorrow and the tears which he has prescribed for me.... I had hoped that this innocent wish [the double union of the houses of Habsburg and Lorraine] would be the consolation of my old age, but God has decreed otherwise.[13]

In grief she made another gain: Van Swieten became another of the men around Maria Theresa.[14] A Catholic, born in Leiden and raised in an atmosphere heavily laced with Jansenism, Van Swieten studied at both Louvain and Leiden. A student of Herman Boerhave, the most eminent medical teacher of the day, Van Swieten had an established practice and a growing reputation for his scholarship when Maria Theresa first invited him to become imperial court physician in 1743. He had declined, but when Maria Anna fell ill Kaunitz had summoned him to Brussels. Despite his failure to save the archduchess, the tenderness with which he treated his patient convinced Maria Theresa that he must come to Vienna. Maria Anna's death intensified her concern that members of her family must have the best medical attention possible. Consequently, she made an offer Van Swieten could not resist: he came both as court physician and court librarian. Proceeding from those offices Van Swieten would play an important role in subsequent domestic reforms. A contentious, sober man, Van Swieten was pragmatic and active rather than philosophical and reflective—well-fitted to serve his new mistress.

The emergence of such new men signified the development of

a distinctly Theresian court life. To be sure, many of the trappings remained unchanged, but there was a new quality in the atmosphere. At the least, the transformation from an imperial to a queenly court was quickly apparent. The dowager-empress sought to maintain certain niceties of imperial ceremonial and courtiers like Khevenhüller-Metsch aided her, but Maria Theresa's own disregard for formalities left its mark as the frequent lamentations of Khevenhüller-Metsch in the pages of his diary make plain. Even after the court regained imperial status, the strict etiquette of the past did not return.

Don Manuel Tellez de Menezes e Castro, Duke of Sylva, Count Tarouca, a Portuguese noble who had served in the administration of the Netherlands under Charles VI and who was chosen by Maria Theresa to serve as her social conscience, observed with obvious disapproval that she spent little time at her toilette.[15] She had no use for the French liturgy of the dressing chamber, but dressed and ate quickly in order to permit a short visit to the nursery before beginning her work. Sylva-Tarouca was mortified that she drank her coffee hot! He was ultimately able to convince her of the folly (or impropriety) of some of her ways, and her increasing abstention from the lighter family entertainments she had enjoyed early in her reign resulted in part from his oddly puritanical influence (and in part from her reaction to Francis' over-zealous attention to other ladies who might be present) but she never returned to the regimen of Spanish court protocol. Much has been made of Sylva-Tarouca's role.[16] Indeed Maria Theresa charged him "to show me my faults and make me recognize them" and insisted, "Always speak forcefully, for even if I do not immediately follow your advice your words will later bring me to my senses."[17] She confided in him about personal matters and there developed an intimacy between them that appeared suggestive to some uninformed observers. Judging by her reactions to his comments about her behavior, his actual influence was slight. He appears to have been a receptacle for her confidences rather than an adviser. Strikingly, to those who knew her most intimately, Francis and Sylva-Tarouca, she conceded little authority, while from those who served her most ably as advisers and ministers she remained personally distant.

In retrospect she observed:

Bartenstein and Haugwitz gave me what I needed for the State and the preservation of the Monarchy. Tarouca and Koch [secretary to the cabinet since 1740, in effect her private secretary] supplied me with consolation, counsel and private information for my own knowledge and correction; and so long as I live I shall be mindful of them, their children, and their children's children for the services which they rendered to me and the State.[18]

With clay of her own choosing Maria Theresa was molding her own regime. By 1748 many of the aged counselors she had inherited had died or retired. Calling on her new counselors, Maria Theresa resolved to reexamine Austria's situation, both externally and internally. The tentative and incomplete nature of the changes made prior to 1749 reflect the basic premises of the great reform, but Maria Theresa clearly recognized the early reforms for what they were. Conscious of how close to destruction the monarchy had been, how weak its means of resistance, she prepared to use the peace to reconstruct her inheritance. With the end of the war in 1748, Maria Theresa had concluded her apprenticeship.

CHAPTER IV

Theresian Reforms: Domestic Policy

FROM 1745 MARIA THERESA HAD EAGERLY ANTICIPATED THE moment of peace when she could take up the task she regarded as the most urgent need of her monarchy: the fundamental reform of the government. Like the emergency measures of the war years, however, the great reforms of 1749 had as their fundamental motive—at least for Maria Theresa—an essentially pragmatic rather than philosophical base. She was convinced that her lands must have the strength to prevent future aggressions of the kind that had deprived her of Silesia. Though not reconciled to that loss, she understood the imperative need to reorganize her inheritance in light of it: if Silesia were to be regained, the monarchy must be stronger without its resources than it had been with them.

The lost province was more than an object of the reforms; it provided the basic model for them. The man who authored the new system, Friedrich Wilhelm Count Haugwitz, had first served the House of Habsburg in Breslau and subsequently closely observed the Prussian reorganization in Silesia after the conquest. Friedrich Walter, in his monumental study of Theresian administrative history, characterizes the Haugwitzian phase of the reforms as being rooted in Austrian theory and Prussian practice.[1] In essence, the Prussian reform in Silesia was an extension of the innovations made throughout the Hohenzollern dominions under Frederick William I.[2] The fact that the Prussians extracted much more from the province in requisitions and taxes than the Austrians had ever done, yet in the process met no resistance from the local estates, particularly intrigued Haugwitz. He intended to leave this system unaltered should Silesia be restored to its rightful ruler. Impressed by the capabilities of the Prussian provincial structure, Haugwitz looked beyond local limits to consider the example of the central administration.

There too he found much to admire, although he saw the need to adjust the lessons learned to the realities of the Austrian situation.

Haugwitz was not bringing the Prussian example into a vacuum, for in fact the attitudes and principles, commonly identified by the term "cameralism," by which the Prussian reforms had been explained and around which they were ordered, had found their fullest expression among a group of Austrian theoreticians—men such as Johann Joachim Becher (1625-1685), Wilhelm von Schroder (1640-1688), and Philipp Wilhelm von Hörnigk (1638-1712). In the simplest terms, cameralism refers to mercantilism in its German expression. This expression is differentiated from other mercantilist forms because only in the German states did the establishment of an economic policy identifiable with mercantilism coincide with the process of political centralization. (This is not to say that a relationship between mercantilism and centralization did not exist elsewhere, for indeed it did, but nowhere else did they so closely coincide.) Becher, Schroder and Hörnigk are commonly identified as the principal exponents of early cameralism and their ideas had a profound influence on the Austrian and Prussian leaders of the eighteenth century. Even before Haugwitz's time an Austrian government official, Christian Julius von Schierendorff (1661-1726), had attempted to introduce cameralist ideas in the Austrian administration, but his attempts resulted only in a series of proposals and memoranda which had no immediate effect, although they would be reexamined in the 1750's and 1760's. In contrast to Schierendorff, who was principally influenced by Becher's emphasis on the internal relations between the component parts of the monarchy, Haugwitz received his inspiration from Schroder who had emphasized princely absolutism. Schroder had declared that his goal could be attained by the creation of a standing army and the possession of a full treasury; to this prescription Haugwitz clearly acceded. The stress of both the theoretician and the reformer on a strong unitary administration bordered on and at times was identical with theocratic absolutism. Though sharing only the generalized convictions of cameralism and not the theoretical foundations, Maria Theresa readily absorbed the projects of reform that derived from them. The bitter experience of having to beg her own domains for help and the sense of having been called by God to dynastic leadership prepared her to accept the idea of centralization.

The core of Haugwitz's reforms was the establishment of a single authority encompassing both political and financial administration. This new authority would submerge the chancelleries, the instrument of estate particularism. By 1744 he had begun to implement his proposals in Austrian Silesia. Impressed by the results, Maria Theresa transferred him to Carniola and Carinthia (1747) to enact similar measures. He had hardly completed his work there when she called him to a greater task: the establishment of a uniform and centralized military system.

The military organization of the monarchy was an accurate reflection of the pervasive provincialism. The estates of each province were responsible for raising and maintaining whatever troops were necessary for that province.[3] As a consequence, the estates were reluctant to levy troops except when their province was directly threatened. The ease with which Prussia had overrun Silesia and then Bohemia at the beginning of the war suggests the inadequacy of this system—as does the erratic character of the Austrian war effort through the remainder of the war. In light of this experience, Haugwitz recommended the creation of a standing army under the direct supervision of the monarch, with a peacetime strength of 180,000, and maintained by an annual military budget of almost fifteen million gulden, compared to the less than nine million previously supplied by the estates.

Dissent quickly appeared, with Harrach and Count Philipp Kinsky providing the most persuasive voices. In their opposition they embodied a concern earlier expressed by Khevenhüller who decried "the unfortunate spirit of innovation, which appeared soon after the death of Charles VI and daily increased," and the "total upheaval and restyling of the . . . form of government."[4] Specifically, their objection was not military but political: they saw this reform as a serious blow to the power of the estates, the stronghold of the old landed families. In resisting the change on this ground, they were indeed striking at the real significance of Haugwitz's military program. The military advantages were undeniable, but most importantly the reorganization would extend state control because Haugwitz's recommendation required the centralization of power. In response to Haugwitz's proposals, Harrach offered a plan which would have placed control over military finances in the hands of the estates. The issue was

clearly drawn between the central authority and the authority
of the estates.

The State Conference began to consider the alternate plans
on January 29, 1748. Maria Theresa later asserted that the Conference unanimously defeated Harrach's proposal and so adopted
Haugwitz's proposal.[5] The proceedings of the Conference indi-
cate, however, that only Khevenhüller supported Haugwitz, and
even he did not accept the political implications of the reform,
arguing solely on grounds of military efficiency. Maria Theresa
herself made the decision to adopt Haugwitz's plan and even
before the Conference met she had accepted both the particular
measures and broader implications of those measures. Maria
Theresa did not crave power, but she sought to guarantee the
present safety and future welfare of the lands with which she
had been entrusted, and for this the "estatism" advocated by
Harrach and Kinsky and accepted by the other ministers largely
from fear of change had already proven woefully inadequate.

Almost immediately she commissioned Haugwitz to go to
Bohemia and Moravia, now the most important provinces in the
monarchy, to prepare for the implementation of his reform. She
hoped that the new military system would take effect on November 1, 1748. Opposition to the change persisted, however, now
on the provincial level.

The estates, in their resistance, operated on the basis of legal
rights in many cases, but Maria Theresa was convinced that a
higher law, public and state interest, justified her. In this conviction, Maria Theresa appealed especially to a divinely ordained
equality: her absolute obligation to protect equally the necessary and hard-earned rights and responsibilities of each element
of society. Therefore she did not reject out of hand the privileges
of the estates, but observed that had the estates served better
the welfare of the society she would willingly have extended
their privileges. Precisely because the estates had used their
prerogatives for the advancement of their own interests rather
than for the good of society, she felt forced to act. Maria Theresa
had already displayed her determination in the meetings of the
Privy Conference. She had advised Harrach that he should carefully reconsider his position and either support his monarch or
"travel to Spaa" (that is, she would send him on a mission that
would remove him from Vienna). In fact, both Harrach and
Kinsky found it advisable to withdraw from public service. In

the provincial administrations, others found it advisable to retire.

Maria Theresa's firmness in supporting his program encouraged Haugwitz to advocate a general reform of the state. On May 2, 1749, the queen issued a declaration which asserted as the basic guide for the ordering of the state the principle of centralization. In place of the two chanceries, Bohemian and Austrian, Maria Theresa established a single Central Directory. Throughout the monarchy she created a series of district councils to serve as the main link between the countryside and the monarchy. At the same time she recognized as an integral part of the system the separation of powers alluded to as early as 1745: not the Central Directory, but a High Court of Justice would inherit the judicial supervision which the chanceries formerly exercised. The separation and centralization of judicial matters brought into the open the vast differences in law and judicial custom among the various parts of the monarchy and subsequently encouraged attempts to codify and rationalize the entire legal system. Work on that perplexing problem began in 1753 with the establishment of a commission to codify civil law in the German provinces and continued throughout Maria Theresa's reign, though with only minimal success. In discussions regarding the codification of law, Maria Theresa tried to mute the conflict between advocates of state absolutism and proponents of the rule of law. She failed because she did not wish to depart too radically from traditional legal and political ideas and thus could not adopt the alternative which jusnaturalism offered. Even so, the working out of details was anticlimactic: Maria Theresa had already revolutionized the constitution by creating the Directory and the High Court of Justice.

To be sure the revolution was not as thorough as Haugwitz would have desired. In the first place Hungary was exempted from many of the major changes. By the settlement of 1741 Maria Theresa had guaranteed certain "rights, liberties, immunities and prerogatives" to the Hungarian Estates. In the matter of tax reforms she observed: "Only in the Kingdom of Hungary did I think it better not to introduce any change, because it would have been inadvisable to attempt anything of the sort except at a legally convoked Diet, and special considerations apply in the case of the Hungarians, who are extremely sensitive on such points."[6] Specifically, she had exempted the

Hungarian nobility from taxation, but the particularity of the Hungarian situation included more than tax exemptions and the Hungarian Estates were indeed "extremely sensitive." Only in foreign affairs, defense, and matters related directly to crown lands was Hungary integrated with the rest of the monarchy. Royal power was not inconsiderable as a result, still Hungary's historic particularism tempered it. In the second place, the enactment of reforms in the non-Hungarian lands was not absolutely uniform. The reorganization of the provincial administrations, a crucial facet of the growth of royal power, varied from province to province. These variations resulted in part from the differing local conditions, but Maria Theresa's pragmatic attitude toward reform tended to reinforce these differences.

By 1749, the opposition to Haugwitz seemed to have been effectively stilled. On the one hand, Maria Theresa's enthusiasm for the reform brooked no opposition, and on the other, the deaths in 1749 of both Kinsky and Harrach removed the most articulate voices of dissent. Even so, doubts about the new system persisted among a majority of the landed nobility and in the upper echelons of the bureaucracy. The bureaucrats, while approving of the purpose behind Haugwitz's proposals, nonetheless questioned whether the particular reforms were appropriate and viewed with special concern the increase in the Directory's authority. While the bureaucratic critics were strange bedfellows for those of the nobility who condemned the purpose itself, bedfellows they were, forming a significant bloc of opposition that awaited an opportunity to renew the attack (an opportunity that did not finally come until Austria was again in the midst of war). This bloc found a negative bond of unity in their dislike of the "system" and until the system was set aside they managed to cling together. Eminently typical of the bureaucratic response was Bartenstein. Though clearly sympathetic to centralization and an active participant in the efforts to create the Haugwitzian system, he was also conscious of its flaws, and recognized the danger of the dissatisfaction over the reforms among crucial elements of the population. In 1753, he asserted that not only the nobility, but the clergy, the military, the burghers, and the peasants were discontented. Discontent among the nobility and the landed clergy was to be expected, but that the other groups were dissatisfied seems surprising since the reforms worked to their advantage. Bartenstein identified the source of unrest as the general uneasiness and insecurity created by so profound an alteration of the polity. The persistence of such unrest he saw as dangerous for the monarchy itself.

The new system was strikingly successful in certain ways. A comparison of the revenues gathered from the various provinces for military expenditures in 1739 and in 1763 reveals that in spite of the loss of Silesia, the source of thirty-five percent of the military subsidy in 1739, the total revenue in 1763 increased by almost sixty-five percent.[7] But the opponents of the system were ready to identify and magnify any flaw. To be sure, the system, having been premised upon a complete revolution at the core of the polity, was bound to have flaws, was bound in a sense to be incomplete. The queen herself, for all her determined support of Haugwitz, could not accept one logical ramification of his system: the establishment of an administrative order based entirely on ability and service. Her conception of society was aristocratic and within any political structure there had to be room for the continued exercise of aristocratic privileges. She had no intention of abdicating power to the aristocracy, but she was as opposed to any undue infringement of noble privileges as she was to any unfounded claim of noble prerogatives. Her conception of society thus placed certain limitations on the rationalization of state power.

One source of weakness in the new system appears to have been Haugwitz himself. Friend and foe alike characterized him as a superlative organizer and a less than satisfactory administrator. Count Johann Chotek, an avowed enemy of Haugwitz, enthusiastically approved the system as the means of solidifying and strengthening the power of the state, but deplored the tremendous cost of the apparatus: Khevenhüller-Metsch had observed quite early Haugwitz's inability to cope with the problems of fiscal administration. Not until the fires of war tested Haugwitz and his system, however, were their frailties fully apparent.

The great reform of 1749 affected all aspects of society. The basic objectives remained constant: economic improvement, centralization of power, and the welfare of the people. And in all things the personal touch of the monarch left its imprint. In confronting the financial difficulties of her dominions, a persistent concern, Maria Theresa almost instinctively recognized that a mere reordering of the antiquated tax system (admittedly in desperate need of reform) was not enough.[8] The bureaucratic solution, to rationalize the fiscal structure, dealt only with the incidence of taxation, not with the more basic and human issue of the general poverty of the population. Maria Theresa saw through to that issue and so assumed as functions of government the improvement of conditions among the peasantry and the protection of the peasants from the excessive demands of the landowners. Thus the reorganization of the provincial administrations, the first phase of the Haugwitzian program, was not only an aspect of political centralization, but also of agrarian reform. By depriving the lords of administrative functions and transforming the district officers from agents of the estates to agents of the crown, Maria Theresa established a direct line of authority between monarch and serf. On the basis of this authority, she intervened into the lord-serf relationship to a degree unknown in most European countries. To further her aims Maria Theresa carried out a new land survey intended to distinguish clearly between noble and peasant land, and thus to guard against future noble encroachments of peasant land. She also called for a reduction of peasant dues and services.

While the culmination of agrarian reforms under Joseph II, the abolition of the *robot* and so of serfdom, grew naturally from the Theresian reforms, she never seriously attempted an abolition of all servile obligations. A humanitarian spirit pervaded her reforms, but this spirit was basically maternal and never gave rise to ideological arguments for total emancipation. In 1742, when Charles VII invaded Bohemia, he promised to abolish serfdom in return for peasant support in his campaign. Maria Theresa had considered making a similar vow, but finally had demurred on grounds that the distinction between lord and serf was part of the natural social order. Indeed Charles VII's tampering with that order profoundly disturbed her. Subsequently, in confirming and clarifying the distinction between noble and peasant land, Maria Theresa lightened the tax burden on the peasant, but the tax rate on peasant land remained higher than on noble land. Maria Theresa sought to meet the financial needs of the state and to improve the peasants' lot, but within the framework of the existing order. However, she established two significant precedents: the reforming of servile conditions on state lands and the regulating of manorial relations by the state.[9]

Maria Theresa's advisers were aware that administrative efficiency and tax redistribution would not of themselves solve the monarchy's economic problems. Even population growth, a characteristic formula of eighteenth-century economic thought, was not a panacea. They had also to encourage long-range economic growth that would enable the taxpayers to meet their obligations, and indeed to bear still heavier ones. Necessarily then, the government had to develop commercial and industrial policies that would increase productivity.

The major goals of Austrian economic policy after 1750 were to free the monarchy from dependence on foreign suppliers and to create a more prosperous population. The loss of Silesia, the most heavily industrialized province in the monarchy and at the same time the principal commercial intermediary between Austria and the outside world, complicated the effort to attain those goals, for it made necessary a major reorientation of commerce and a vigorous promotion of industry. For two decades the government pursued a policy of "relatively dogmatic mercantilism."[10] The government then frequently intervened, but not indiscriminately. Intervention was not a doctrinaire policy. Maria Theresa herself ordered the Commercial Council to recommend whatever measures were necessary, but in fact the Council regularly favored indirect rather than direct measures.

Indicative of government policy was the treatment of the guilds. In 1751 Maria Theresa considered the possibility of abolishing the guilds, but finally and characteristically refrained from so drastic a step. She did, however, attempt to reduce the restrictive powers they exercised. She decreed that guilds dealing in commodities for local consumption were free to function without interference so long as they adequately supplied the population. The government watched the balance of supply and demand to prevent the creation of artificial shortages. In contrast, the "commercial crafts" whose products supplied national or international markets, were to be opened to full competition, with the government being responsible for standards of workmanship. But the craftsmen were slow to take to the new ways and Maria Theresa found it very difficult to change the traditional attitudes and procedures of the guilds. When she imported foreign artisans, the native masters refused to accept them. To encourage the production of "fine cloth" the government promised immediate purchase by the army of all that was produced, but no one responded to the offer. A prize competition for cloth received only one entry.

Even more dilatory than the craftsmen were the Habsburg merchants. Despite a concerted effort to establish a "Buy Habsburg" policy, the merchants continued to purchase admittedly cheaper and better foreign goods. Furthermore, the merchants were not willing to invest in native industry although the government's plans depended on such investment. The persistent refusal of the merchant community to cooperate was a major reason for the lack of industrial progress during this period. Confronted by this obstinacy, the government tried to force the purchase of domestic goods, or alternatively to ban imports, but with little result. Ironically, the nobility was far more willing to invest in native industry and to support government policy, but despite governmental subsidies most of the manorial industrial units were unsuccessful. Government-established industries were hardly more productive. Significantly the government clearly favored small-scale, local industries, presumably the kind which would have the most immediate benefits for the peasantry, that is the large bulk of Maria Theresa's people.[11]

Perhaps less obvious, though no less important, than Maria Theresa's industrial and commercial policies for strengthening the state and improving the lot of the people, was her educational policy. From quite early in her reign, Maria Theresa sought to improve education in her lands, though her motives were pragmatic rather than intellectual. She tended to judge all intellectual endeavor in terms of the material benefits it bestowed on the society, and thus had little tolerance for independent thought and creativity. Even Arneth, who was generally quite sympathetic toward Maria Theresa, was critical of this propensity. Noting regretfully that Austria had not been productive soil for scholarship, Arneth added that at least part of the blame must be ascribed to the attitudes of the ruler.[12]

Maria Theresa's first efforts at educational reform, like her other early programs, had been tentative and directed to specific matters without reference to any master plan for education. The educational needs of the state worked against the creation of a uniform system. Reform at the university level could be and was directed toward the training of civil servants, but a universal system of education in which all members of the society would have the possibility of such service opened to them was not compatible with Maria Theresa's social conceptions. She advocated universal education, but intended a system which would provide each social estate with the education appropriate to it. Thus, for the lower classes there was to be a general elementary education in which the instruction would be limited to those things necessary to live adequately and happily as a member of those classes. To Maria Theresa this meant not necessarily the basic rudiments of reading, writing, and arithmetic, but the cultivation of piety and virtue and the development of technical skills. In particular, she desired to divest popular religion of the remnants of folk superstitions, to purify the faith of the people. To accomplish this, various prohibitions were established, but Maria Theresa recognized that mere prohibitions would not suffice, that a positive effort to educate the population in orthodoxy was necessary.

The fullest and most concerted effort to improve popular education would come in the last decade of her reign. During the earlier period, the greatest advances were made in the establishment or improvement of special institutions, such as the Theresianum, where sons of the nobility were trained for royal service, or the University of Vienna. Especially significant was the development of the medical school in Vienna under the guidance of Gerhard Van Swieten. Maria Theresa in 1749 requested him to propose a plan of reorganization for medical education. She accepted his proposal and in effect gave him supervisory authority over all aspects of medical education in Austria. Subsequently, the principles of his reform were extended to the other faculties of the university. Here in microcosm was repeated the common pattern of Theresian reform.

In essence Van Swieten's proposal removed control of the university from the faculty and placed it in the hands of a court-appointed official. This innovation, as alarming as it might be to a modern academic community, freed legal curricula from the narrow strictures of ecclesiastical control. Even the philosophical and theological curricula were released from subjection to the rigidity of Jesuit censorship. In this matter, as in others, Van Swieten demonstrated a persistent and deep disdain for the Jesuits. In spite of that attitude which she most certainly did not share, Maria Theresa endorsed and encouraged Van Swieten's proposals because they were clearly consistent with her own policy of restricting any special interest which threatened royal rights or obstructed her efforts to benefit her people.

Not unrelated to the great tasks of reform was the education of her children—a matter that grew no simpler because in peace as in war the family circle continued to grow: Johanna Gabriella, born February 4, 1750; Maria Josepha, born May 19, 1751; Maria Caroline, born August 13, 1752; Ferdinand Karl, born June 1, 1754; Marie Antoinette, born November 2, 1755; and finally Maximilian Franz, born December 8, 1756. Amidst all the other demands on her time Maria Theresa found opportunity to prepare elaborate instructions for the care and training of each of her children and even to supervise that training. There was always to be time in her schedule to visit the nursery or the parlor, but the duties of monarchy constantly impinged even on that private world. Her concern for her children's education was not purely maternal, but derived from her consciousness of the future roles they would play, as rulers or as royal wives. In this regard she especially attended to the education of her oldest son and heir, Joseph. Some historians have suggested that she was too ardent in her supervision, but she was too acutely aware of the greater magnitude of his future responsibilities and of the unfortunate neglect of her own education to respond in any other way. The spirit and substance of the training she desired for her son are readily apparent in the instructions she prepared for Field Marshal Count Karl Batthyány, whom she appointed in 1751 to superintend Joseph's education.[13] (The appointment itself reflected Maria Theresa's unrelenting political consciousness: in 1751 Maria Theresa was again embroiled in difficulties with the Hungarian Diet; Batthyány not only bore a good Hungarian name, but his brother succeeded Palffy as Count Palatine of Hungary in 1751.)

Religion played a central part in the educational process she prescribed:

Each day must begin with prayer and the first and most necessary thing for my son is to be certain with a submissive heart of God's omnipotence, to love and to fear Him, and to develop from true Christian practice and duty all other virtues.[14]

Maria Theresa believed that the practice of piety was beneficial and so required daily attendance at mass, regular confession, and the reading of pious works. Conscious that she lived in a century of free thought, she sought to protect her children from dangerous influences by empowering their confessor to censor everything they read.

In the regimen for Joseph, Maria Theresa also stressed the study of language. Thus he was well versed in the classics and in addition learned French, Italian, Magyar, and even a little Bohemian as well as German. The actual director of academic studies was Bartenstein who for the occasion prepared a massive history of Europe with the purpose of acquainting the archduke with the histories of each of the various dominions he was to inherit and who rigorously examined him, sometimes in the presence of Maria Theresa. That this aspect of Joseph's training was less than successful resulted from his own particular nature and the sheer pedantry of his tutor.

More important were Maria Theresa's efforts to introduce Joseph to the practical problems of statecraft. She employed various experts to prepare detailed political and statistical analyses of the imperial states for his perusal. The two documents which she herself wrote and which are commonly referred to as her "Political Testament" were undoubtedly intended as guidebooks for her heir. As early as 1761 he regularly attended meetings of the Council of State, and then submitted reports of his thoughts and observations to his mother. This introduction to the complexities of government was accompanied by an emphasis on the ideal of the monarch's relationship with his subjects implicit in Maria Theresa's love for her people.

Finally, Joseph was steeped in the military profession. Batthyány was not only a Hungarian but also a military man. In that regard too the choice was purposeful—Maria Theresa may well have been commenting on the military deficiencies of her predecessors, and Francis as well. Batthyány firmly believed that royal birth per se was not enough, that a prince to be worthy of his calling must excel in all things. Therefore, in things military Joseph's tutors were the best generals Austria possessed at the time. Joseph also read widely in military history and particularly came to admire Julius Caesar, Charles XII of Sweden, and Frederick the Great.

In short, in educating her heir, Maria Theresa, while carrying over certain emphases from her own education, seemed determined to correct the mistakes made in her own preparation for ruling. Similar programs were prepared for Leopold and the

other younger sons. However much the substance of the education of Joseph and his brothers may be criticized, Maria Theresa
gave more attention to the problem of how to educate a monarch than did most of her "enlightened" contemporaries. Having
come to power in the Habsburgs' darkest hour with only her
native wisdom and resolution to sustain her, she meant to provide
Joseph with a thorough apprenticeship. The contrast between
the strict, albeit not harsh, regimen she provided for Joseph
and the more relaxed and disconnected training she received is
at heart the difference between the education of a man born
to rule and the preparation of a monarch's wife.

Maria Theresa had no concern that any of her daughters would
have to bear the manly tasks of government and therefore their
educations were of a different character. Their tutors remarked
of all but one (Maria Christina) that they lacked the ability
to concentrate, a faculty requisite for a monarch, but less necessary for a monarch's wife. If Maria Theresa did not try to correct
this lack it was from conviction and not from carelessness. She
did not intend her daughters to be imitations of herself: that
was not their God-given place in the order of things. They were
to be pious and cultivated companions for kings and princes,
capable of diverting their husbands, of conducting a suitable
household and of mothering a future generation of princes and
princesses. Marie Antoinette's ignorance of governmental and
political realities was regrettable, if not tragic, but Maria Theresa
had no wish to raise an Elizabeth Farnese, or a Catherine II.

In educating her children, particularly her sons, Maria Theresa
did not entirely succeed in warding off "the evil spirits of the
eighteenth century." A new spirit had begun to permeate Europe
and the baroque world in which she had formed her conceptions differed markedly from the milieu in which her children
formed theirs. Symbolic of the change was the nearly simultaneous publication of Montesquieu's *Esprit des Lois* (1748),
Muratori's *Della publica felicita, ogetto di buono principi* (1749),
and the first volume of the *Encyclopédie* (1751).[15] The period
1750-1770, in fact, marked the highpoint of French influence in
Austrian life and the beginning of the Austrian Enlightenment.[16]
Ironically, Maria Theresa's own policy actively encouraged the
shift. In foreign policy, rapprochement with France marked
the period; more importantly, the erosion, then the elimination,
of Jesuit control over censorship opened the gates of Vienna to

the western winds. Maria Theresa herself had directly intervened in the controversy over Montesquieu and had ordered
the publication of *Esprit des Lois* in Austria (1753). To be
sure, censorship continued but she appointed Van Swieten
president of the censorship commission and while he cannot be
regarded as an Enlightenment man, he was enlightened. Maria
Theresa could and did overrule him on occasion. (She had
a particular distaste for satire: "As far as I am concerned, I dislike everything that one might call irony. Nobody is ever made
better by it—only irritated—and I regard it as incompatible with
love for our neighbor.")[17] Yet the standards Van Swieten set
for censorship were freer than those previously applied and
freer than one would expect given the biases of the queen.

Within the body politic the Enlightenment had two facets: the
introduction of rational principles into a basically authoritarian
philosophy and the almost simultaneous permeation of government by the humanitarian spirit.[18] The philosophical objectives
of the Enlightenment probably penetrated Austria more slowly
than almost anywhere else, but the practical application of the
humanitarian tendencies appeared in Austria earlier than in
many of the philosophically "more progressive" states. Many
historians have argued that in terms of the humanitarian ideal
Theresian Austria was more enlightened than any other European
country of the eighteenth century. The vital characteristic of the
Austrian Enlightenment was its empirical bent: reforms were
not based on a rationalized concept of the "popular will" or on
the assumption of a "social contract," but on the recognition of
observable need. In theory this placed Theresian Austria closer
to the Austria of Charles VI but in its accomplishments only
Josephian Austria is comparable. The explanation of this circum-
stance is quite simply the pervasive and particular impact of one
person, Maria Theresa. The pragmatic and humane dimensions
of Austrian government in the mid-eighteenth century were as
much if not more reflective of her personality than of the new
wisdom of the age.

CHAPTER V

Theresian Reforms:
The Diplomatic Revolution

THE "DIPLOMATIC REVOLUTION" WAS A SERIES OF REALIGNMENTS and agreements in 1755-1756 culminating in an alliance between the traditional "natural enemies," Austria and France, Habsburgs and Bourbons. Historians dispute whether this shift in the European system was a sudden shift caused by a particular cluster of events after 1754, a reaction to the tensions created among the various allies at the peace negotiations in Aix-la-Chapelle (1748), or a product of a long, though erratic, development dating back to the reign of Louis XIV.[1] In any case, the realignment completed one facet of the project to which Maria Theresa had dedicated herself as early as the Treaty of Dresden (1745), the transformation of the system on which Habsburg dynastic power had been based; the realignment then was an integral part of the great Theresian reforms.

A comparison of the two memoranda which compose Maria Theresa's Political Testament offers some insights into the relationship between domestic and foreign policy. Both emphasize the disorder in the monarchy's internal administration at the time of Maria Theresa's accession, but the earlier document, written amidst the great reforms of 1749-1750, hardly mentions foreign relations at all, while the later document, written during the Diplomatic Revolution, regards those relations as critical.[2] Maria Theresa was conscious of the importance of foreign affairs at all times, but she was equally conscious that a complete reorientation of Austria's alliance system was possible only when the monarchy had regained sufficient strength to be an attractive ally. Thus in 1749-1750 internal reorganization had first priority. Nevertheless, she did not neglect to lay the groundwork for an external reorganization.

[78]

Having concluded during the war that the traditional alliance with the maritime powers was inadequate because it failed to provide sufficient support against Prussia, Maria Theresa had pressed for a separate accommodation with France at Aix-la-Chapelle and she was quick to forgive French duplicity when the effort failed. Increasingly she relied on Kaunitz for diplomatic advice because he shared with her a preference for rapprochement with France and she pursued that goal without qualm although her husband remained a central figure of the anti-French clique at the Vienna court. Maria Theresa had no intention of making precipitous commitments. What she intended was a reconstruction of Austria's alliance system based on a critical assessment of all the problems and possibilities confronting the monarchy: that was the other half of the State Conference's task in 1749.[3]

The crucial discussions on foreign affairs occurred in March-April, 1749, when each of the Conference members (of whom Kaunitz was the newest, and youngest) submitted a formal written statement to Maria Theresa. Much later, Kaunitz commented that the three possible courses of action were: to strengthen the alliance with the maritime powers and Russia on the basis of the mutual opposition to France; to alienate France from her principal ally, Prussia, without either withdrawing from the alliance with England and the Netherlands or entering a full alliance with France; or to separate from the traditional alliance and to ally with the Bourbons.[4] From these alternatives Maria Theresa had to choose, though she had told Bartenstein she would follow the course favored by the majority of the Conference.

All the Conference members agreed that Austria could not fight both France and Prussia. Previously, pressure from England had forced Austria to solve this dilemma by neutralizing Prussia in order to continue the conflict against France, but now Maria Theresa's counselors agreed that the monarchy had to neutralize France in order to defend itself against Prussia. In his memorandum Kaunitz raised the possibility of receiving direct or indirect aid from France and in so doing came close to advocating the alliance system as it finally materialized in 1756, but he did not press this proposal as an immediate alternative. Rather, on the basis of the existing situation, he recommended a policy of avoiding all conflict with England and with France while working

toward the diplomatic isolation of Prussia.[5] On that he agreed
with the majority of his colleagues, but much more emphatically
than they he stressed the inadequacy of the traditional alliance
and the permanence of the conflict with Prussia. These emphases
he shared with Maria Theresa. And, as in the case of Haugwitz
in internal affairs, Maria Theresa found in Kaunitz an architect
for policies to fulfill her goals. For that reason, in 1750 she dispatched him to Versailles as Austrian ambassador to the court of
Louis XV.

In her instructions to both Kaunitz and Count Richecourt, the
Austrian ambassador to England, Maria Theresa assumed the
maintenance of the alliance with the sea powers, but she fervently
reiterated the idea that they must convince France of her fervent
desire for peace. She specifically charged Richecourt to seek
a renewed guarantee of the Treaty of Dresden, especially the
clauses protecting Austria from aggression, and English adherence to the Austro-Russian alliance of 1746. Of these she regarded
the latter aim as more crucial. Though the 1746 treaty was
primarily a defensive alliance to protect Austria from attack
either by Turkey or by Prussia, Maria Theresa had had long-
term expectations for it as evidenced by the fact that she had
asked Elizabeth to be godparent to her third son (born in 1747)
and named him Peter Leopold after the tsarina's father. Even
so, she continued to view the agreement as a defensive arrangement, for otherwise she would hardly have sought English adherence to it, since she was well aware that England would
never become party to such an offensive alliance against Prussia.
To be sure, England was not invited to accede to certain secret
articles whose implications were injurious to Prussia, but even
these articles did not change the agreement's basically defensive
nature. What Maria Theresa intended, and what she believed she
had accomplished by England's accession to the treaty in
October, 1750, was a further separation of England from Prussia.
The total isolation of Prussia was clearly the object.

Simultaneously, the English were pressing another issue affect-
ing Austrian policy: the election of the Archduke Joseph as King
of the Romans and thus as virtual heir to the imperium.[6] The
chief advocate of the election, the Duke of Newcastle, regarded
the election as a means of guaranteeing the stability of the
empire and more importantly of strengthening the "old system"
since he believed Maria Theresa could not fail to be grateful

for English support of something which had to be so close to
her heart. The failure of the campaign to secure Joseph's election
underlines Maria Theresa's commitment to the policy of trying
to avoid conflict with both England and France while concentrat-
ing her attention on the isolation of Prussia. She did yearn for the
election of Joseph, both as a means of avoiding a repetition of the
chaos of 1740-1742 and of giving dignity to her well-loved son,
but she would not permit these considerations to thwart her
efforts to draw France away from Prussia. The English themselves
were obviously intent on weakening French influence within the
empire, and, whether purposefully or not, they also complicated
greatly the efforts of Kaunitz at Versailles. Already irritated by
the warmth of Austro-Russian relations, the French did not take
kindly to the campaign to press the election.

Maria Theresa's dilemma was simple: if she openly endorsed
the English proposal, she would anger France and thus both
restrengthen the Franco-Prussian relationship and leave herself
dependent on the alliance with England; if she repudiated the
proposal she would alienate England and thus isolate herself
at a time when the Franco-Prussian alliance seemingly remained
in effect. After some delay she informed the English that she
would summon the electors only if the French would acquiesce.
Essentially this stratagem was meant to delay action until either
French approval could be acquired, thus gaining the advantages
of the election without antagonizing the French, or the English
would drop the matter of their own accord, thus not injuring
Anglo-Austrian relations. The latter finally occurred, though not
without strain to the alliance.

In 1753 Maria Theresa appointed Kaunitz as State Chancellor.
With that appointment Maria Theresa both completed one aspect
of administrative reform begun some years before and set the
stage for the great diplomatic transformation of mid-decade. At
the time of Kaunitz's return from Versailles, however, the
goal of isolating Prussia by dissolving her alliance with France
seemed further from attainment than ever. Austria herself in 1752-
1753 found it necessary to reassert the alliance with the maritime
powers. To Maria Theresa, however, this was but a momentary
expediency, an expediency that must have been quite distasteful,
for it was accompanied by new proof of the alliance's inadequacies, the failure to resolve differences between Austria and the
United Netherlands in the Low Countries.[7] Austria's inability to

separate France from Prussia clearly indicated the major flaw in Habsburg policy: the assumption that France could be separated from Prussia without first accomplishing a reconciliation between Austria and France. The separation had become an end in itself and in pursuing that end the Austrians had sought to maintain their own security by preserving the old alliances. France, however, had likewise to look after her security and thus could not reject her former ally unless a suitable replacement was found. While Maria Theresa, Kaunitz, and Bartenstein were able to see this and therefore to see the necessity of making more explicit advances to France, there were many at the Viennese court, including Francis, who could not think in such terms. With the court divided, Austrian policy remained tentative and thus had no appeal in France, where advocates of the old system were also strong. When Maria Theresa appointed Kaunitz State Chancellor, she gave him a double task of education to perform: the education of Vienna as well as Versailles.

At least with Kaunitz's appointment divided opinions no longer weakened government policy, but the new ministry did not suddenly display increased affection for the French. On the contrary, from 1753 to 1755, the emphasis on good relations with England persisted, even Frederick II observing that Kaunitz appeared to be one of those who favored closer relations with the British. Both Maria Theresa and Kaunitz, however, were still intent on dissolving the Franco-Prussian alliance and both regarded this period as a mere interlude, preparatory to carrying out the French project. French reluctance, not Austrian policy, made the interlude necessary. By 1755, however, conditions seemed favorable for the fulfillment of the project. A new colonial war between England and France was already underway and England's maritime superiority made a Continental diversion an attractive strategic alternative for France. In June, 1755, Kaunitz set forth his plan before the Austrian ministry.[8] The memorandum justifying the plan accurately reflected the lessons which he and Maria Theresa felt they had learned in recent years: that Prussia was the cause for all of Austria's greatest problems, that the maritime alliance was not and never would be sufficient to protect Austria against the dangers Prussia posed, that Austria could not fight both France and Prussia, and that the French would consider a rapprochement with Austria, but only if it offered them concrete advantages. Within two months the State Conference had approved the proposed rapprochement and negotiations with France began in earnest. (Ironically, Maria Theresa's confinement with another child, her fifteenth, Marie Antoinette, who was destined to be an important instrument of Austro-French relations in the future, momentarily interrupted the negotiations.)

Neither Maria Theresa nor Kaunitz assumed the discussions would be easy, for despite Louis XV's personal dislike and distrust of Frederick, the French regarded the alliance with Prussia as essential and viewed the destruction of Prussia as a serious threat to their own safety. Thus even a guarantee of neutrality in an Austro-Prussian conflict, the objective Maria Theresa and Kaunitz sought, seemed excessive to the French. For all their persuasive powers they made little headway in wooing the French until Frederick II made a grave error of judgment and concluded the Convention of Westminster with England (January, 1756). By that agreement Frederick believed he had preserved himself from war: Russia would not attack him without English support which was now ruled out, and Austria would not attack without Russian or English aid, also now eliminated; his own promise to protect Hanover against France he regarded as idle, because he could restrain France. What he failed to consider was France's emotional reaction to the Convention.

The substance of the agreement was not inimical to French interests, but Louis XV was outraged by Frederick's failure to inform him of his intentions. This outrage had as its immediate consequence the dissolution of the Franco-Prussian alliance. England's willingness to negotiate with the Prussian fiend merely confirmed Maria Theresa's assessment of both powers and Kaunitz happily seized the occasion to spread rumors of secret articles to the Convention specifically aimed against France. France could still have avoided making an absolute choice between Prussia and Austria. What France required was a guarantee of neutrality that would allow her to pursue the struggle with England free of involvement in a Continental war. Clearly Prussia would have preferred to avoid a direct conflict with France, and as late as January, 1756, Maria Theresa would have promised Austrian neutrality at a price less extravagant than a full defensive alliance. Fearful of diplomatic isolation, the French reacted to Prussia's machinations uncritically and so pledged themselves to an alliance system whose purposes were different from and even in opposition to France's needs.[9] By

May 1, 1756, Austria and France had concluded the Treaty of Versailles on conditions favorable to Austria: in return for a promise of neutrality in the English war, Maria Theresa received a promise of aid in the event of attack.

Indisputably Maria Theresa intended to go to war with Prussia to recover Silesia, but Frederick's attack on Saxony in August, 1756, which brought on that war, was not the anticipated result of her policy to that point. Despite the defensive guarantees of the Versailles Treaty, Maria Theresa did not consciously set out to provoke Frederick in order to bring France into the war. Frederick himself was less concerned about the Franco-Austrian alliance than he was about Russian adherence to that alliance. He had made the Convention of Westminster to neutralize Russia and he began a preventive war when he determined that England could not restrain her. Here he had miscalculated again: he assumed the existence of a tightly-knit conspiracy centered in Vienna and attacked to forestall efforts by that conspiracy to make Russia part of its web. In fact the conspiracy was less unified than he imagined, but Russia was already the most eager for war.[10]

Russia, too, reacted angrily to the Westminster Convention, though she directed her anger at England rather than Prussia. In 1755 Russia and England had concluded a subsidy treaty (the lever by which Frederick believed England could control Tsarina Elizabeth) and the courts had just exchanged ratifications of the agreement. Now England had closed an accord whose purpose seemed to be to limit Russia. Maria Theresa and Kaunitz immediately saw an opportunity to strengthen the alliance with Russia. That alliance had played a critical role in all Maria Theresa's considerations after 1749, but she had recognized that the uncertainties of Russian internal affairs made it a tenuous safeguard of Austrian security: Elizabeth had a personal antipathy to Frederick, but the heir to the throne and his wife, Peter and Catherine, were known to be pro-Prussian. There was little evidence from recent Russian history or Elizabeth's personal life style to encourage Maria Theresa to think the tsarina would enjoy a long tenure in office. Still, in 1756, Elizabeth not only seemed in good health, but was positively vigorous in her expressed intention to chastise Frederick. At that point Maria Theresa's main problem was to restrain her fellow empress from precipitous action.

While genuinely disturbed by Russia's eagerness for war, Maria Theresa also feared that over-restraint of Russia might encourage her to fall back on the English alliance. At the same time she had to restrain Russia long enough for the Austro-French bond to be made as firm as possible. After May, 1756, the Russians were actively planning an attack on Prussia. Maria Theresa, heartened by the success of the French negotiations, now seemed as willing as Elizabeth to open hostilities, and asked her ally if she were prepared to initiate the campaign before the year was out. However, Kaunitz, recognizing that the Austrian army was not yet ready, urged caution, and asserted that 1757 would be a better time to act. Repeatedly Kaunitz instructed Esterhazy, Austria's ambassador to Russia, to inform the St. Petersburg government that Austria would not and could not act until she was absolutely sure of France. Furthermore, efforts to secure the collaboration of Saxony, Poland, and Sweden were progressing slowly. Such was the situation when Frederick invaded Saxony (August 29, 1756).

On the basis of information purloined from the Saxon archives, Frederick acted to steal the march on what he assumed was a well-knit conspiracy against him, drawing its chief inspiration from Vienna. Even the information culled from the Dresden archives following his invasion did not alter his conviction. Obviously there was an anti-Prussian conspiracy, but Frederick misunderstood it. Saxony, against whom Frederick directed his preventive war, had not yet fully committed itself to the projected war against Prussia which Russia had promoted at least as vigorously as Austria. Frederick feared Russia, but he attacked when he did in hopes of forcing the issue before Russia had become involved. Thus in justifying his action (in the *Mémoire Raisonné*) he refrained from any condemnations of Russia since, encouraged by England, he continued under the delusion that he could still keep Russia neutral. Furthermore, when Frederick opened the war on August 29 no unified formal offensive alliance against him existed. Ironically, his attack crystallized that alliance. On August 20 France had tentatively agreed to support a force of German mercenaries, to provide a subsidy to Russia, and to accept the results of Austrian negotiations with such powers as Sweden, but no agreement had yet been signed and France had continued to refuse direct participation. Only French fear of Frederick's relationship with England had driven her this far.

Maria Theresa and Elizabeth would have attacked Frederick in the spring of 1757 without direct or indirect support from Louis XV if they were certain of his neutrality, but in face of the Prussian king's aggression Louis now encouraged the idea of an offensive alliance. Kaunitz now hesitated—the fulfillment of the obligations contained in the defensive accord would have satisfied him—but in May, 1757, France committed herself to a full war against Prussia.

The outbreak of the Seven Years' War and the crystallization of the new alliances climaxed the reconstruction of Austria's foreign relations, part of the general reform to which Maria Theresa had dedicated herself as early as 1745. She had not foreseen the precise form the reconstruction would take (though Kaunitz suggested the outline in 1749) and she hardly controlled the course of events. Nevertheless, she set the goals of the monarchy. More precisely, in the period 1748-1756 she proceeded on the conviction that Prussia was her single most dangerous enemy and that the preservation of her monarchy depended on limiting Frederick's ability to do her harm. Secondarily, she still hoped to restore Silesia to its rightful place among her dominions and regarded its recapture as an essential step in defanging the Prussian wolf. Increasingly others, and particularly Kaunitz, influenced the craft of diplomacy, the methods by which Austria's goals were to be reached. This was not an abdication of authority by Maria Theresa, but a mark of her success in reforming the government. The emergence of Kaunitz brought close to completion the process of administrative centralization associated with the great reforms of 1749. The war she had intended to wage against Frederick naturally followed. To Maria Theresa it was a righteous war, a war to protect her family and people. That Frederick struck first only increased the moral indignation with which she set out to have justice done.

Khevenhüller-Metsch had disapprovingly noted as early as 1743 of the "overly despotic ways of the otherwise so praiseworthy woman" and in 1747 Otto Christian Podewils, the Prussian ambassador, had written:

> Upon her accession she discovered the art of winning everybody's admiration and love. Her sex, her handsome appearance, as well as her misfortunes contributed not a little toward the favorable response. . . . She took pains to show herself in the best of lights. Affable, pious, generous, charitable, simple in manner, courageous

and high-minded, she soon conquered the hearts of her subjects. . . .
[But] the praise lavished on her, and her own well-developed
amour propre as well, soon inflated the opinion she had of her
efficiency and talents. She became high-handed, impatient of advice,
and no longer brooked contradiction.[11]

And many years later she condemned herself for having "made
war out of pride."

But that was later when in sorrow she reflected on the sinful-
ness of pride. In 1756 pride seemed a virtue, for through its
compelling call she had reconstructed her depleted inheritance,
had forced Europe to awaken to the new political reality, and
stood ready to chastise her most implacable foe. She was also
approaching forty. The tasks of government squeezed the gaiety
from her own life and as they did she became less considerate
of the diversions others practiced. A minor, but characteristic,
manifestation of Maria Theresa's advancing sobriety were the
activities of the "chastity commission," a special security force
created in 1753 to superintend the moral behavior of the Viennese
(ironically she named Kaunitz its chairman). The numerous anecdotes about the queen's efforts to enforce morality within
her lands, a Sisyphean labor, led one foreign observer to remark
that Maria Theresa too often dealt with matters that were be-
neath her, prompting people to say that she was "great in great
affairs, and little in little ones."[12]

More and more Maria Theresa had absented herself from
family entertainments and the social amenities of the court.
She had also grown quite stout. Francis, always susceptible to
brief flirtations, now became more deeply involved, with Princess
Wilhelmina Auersperg. This liaison, begun in 1755, lasted until
Francis' death. Whatever the precise details of the relationship
(some Habsburg enthusiasts would have it be purely platonic)
Maria Theresa agonized about it and quarrels became more
frequent.[13] That she tolerated the situation, even protesting that
Princess Auersperg was only a family friend, may have resulted
in part from her own feeling that she bore some responsibility for
Francis' infelicities. She later advised one of her companions,
"Let me warn you. Don't marry a man who has nothing to do."[14]
But she had told Francis directly that he must not involve him-
self in matters that he did not understand, that is, the great
issues of reform and diplomacy which consumed her time. The

Theresian monument on the Ring in Vienna aptly illustrates the situation: Maria Theresa sits enthroned, surrounded by her advisers—Kaunitz, Haugwitz, Van Swieten, Daun, but no Francis. If one follows the line of her right hand, one will encounter a statue of Francis, alone, apart, largely ignored. He himself once observed, "The court is over there. I am only a private man."[15]

The private man pursued his private pleasure, retiring frequently to Laxenburg to hunt and to spend his evenings with "la belle Auersperg." Maria Theresa fretted, sometimes fumed, and always put her work first. She was not a private person.

CHAPTER VI

The Seven Years' War and the Last Great Reforms

FREDERICK OF PRUSSIA IS OFTEN CITED AS THE FIRST MONARCH TO recognize and rule in the context of the new political reality, the modern state and the modern system. However, Frederick himself must have quickly understood in the wake of the Austro-French alliance that Maria Theresa too sensed the inadequacies of the political principles on which traditional European statecraft was based.[1] The second Treaty of Versailles (May, 1757) transformed the original accord between Vienna and Versailles into a full-scale offensive alliance and promised a profound alteration of the European state system. Essentially a statement of war aims, the treaty guaranteed Austrian possession of Silesia in return for the cession of the Austrian Netherlands to the Bourbons. The recovery of Silesia would have reestablished Austrian power in the Empire and thereby in Europe. By relinquishing the Netherlands in favor of Silesia, Maria Theresa would have surrendered non-German for German lands and scattered for contiguous provinces, thus reaffirming the spirit and purpose of the great domestic reforms. (Friedrich Meinecke, in his incisive analysis of *raison d'état,* suggested that the desire to consolidate lands into a contiguous whole was a basic principle of the modern as opposed to the dynastic state.)[2] She would also have punished Frederick for his iniquities. But these goals were to be dreams unfulfilled.

Between the allies there was a basic disagreement over strategy. The war for empire between England and France was a vital element in the crisis that burst upon Europe in the mid-1750's. This extra-European conflict shaped both English and French responses to the Continental situation and influenced the Continental powers themselves in other, less direct, ways, but to

[89]

Maria Theresa the war was bound up entirely with the Silesian question and her antipathy toward Frederick, and the overseas war remained quite unreal. Thus from the very beginning she failed to appreciate the French desire to offset their disadvantage against England on the high seas by striking George II's Hanoverian lands. For her, Silesia was the only logical theater of war. Rigidly adhering to her strategic preference, she had insisted that all she desired from France was the financial assistance pledged in 1756. Despite this disagreement, the French court, dominated until May, 1757, by a militant anti-Prussian faction, had irrepressibly insisted on extending its commitment by the second Versailles treaty.[3]

Starhemberg, Austrian ambassador at Versailles, astutely commented that it remained to be seen whether France had the strength to keep her word. The question quickly became whether she even had the will to do so. The Austrian victory at Kolin (June 18, 1757) proved that the Prussians were not invincible and demonstrated the effectiveness of the military reforms carried out between the wars, but the buoyant optimism that ensued evaporated in the wake of the crushing defeats at Rossbach (November 5) and Leuthen (December 5). With the victory at Leuthen, Frederick regained Silesia, never again to relinquish it. More importantly, England increased her aid to Prussia, while French resolution rapidly dwindled. Thereafter Prussian-Hanoverian forces led by Ferdinand of Brunswick and heavily subsidized by England held the French at bay in Westphalia, while the confrontation of Prussia with Austria and Russia became the central facet of the Continental struggle.[4]

Maria Theresa's own resolution weakened and she confided in Stainville, the French ambassador to Vienna, that perhaps the time had come to negotiate with Frederick. In the hands of someone less ardently anti-Prussian than Stainville this confession of weakness would have quickly reached Versailles and perhaps have proven fatal to the alliance. Already the French foreign minister, the Abbé de Bernis, regretted France's commitments on the Continent. With some difficulty Kaunitz persuaded Stainville that Maria Theresa's remark resulted from momentary depression and that Austria had no intention of slackening her war effort or acting without consulting her ally. Indeed, Maria Theresa's depression was only momentary and the best days of the war for her were yet to come, but the spell was symptomatic of a

change in Maria Theresa. The despotic tendency, which Khevenhüller had noted, became sporadic; the impatience with contradiction, which Podewils had observed, softened. She nagged and
prodded her advisers less and seemed to concede more authority
to them. A natural result, perhaps, of the fact that those around
her were now entirely her men, ones she had chosen and encouraged, but there was something else, some shift, however
subtle, which was most clearly reflected in a growing indecision,
the ebbing of the aggressive righteousness that had characterized
her reforms.

In 1756 Maria Theresa had given birth to her sixteenth and last
child, Maximilian. Pregnancy and childbirth had been an almost
annual process for her since 1737 and the related physiological
and psychological adjustments formed a basic cycle of her life.
But her child-bearing days were over and at some point
after 1756 she experienced the inevitable "change of life" which
must have produced further psychological adjustment. The co-
incidence between this climacteric on the one hand and the indecision and uncertainty which increasingly marked her efforts
and the recurring periods of depression which more frequently
lessened her resolution on the other is suggestive. These symp-
toms of psychological distress may well have been more than
simply responses to external developments.

These developments nonetheless had an impact. The military
stalemate on the western front in 1758 produced new strains on
the alliance. French resolution continued to weaken and Maria
Theresa grew more and more suspicious of French intentions.[5]
When the French renewed the debate on strategy she suggested
to Kaunitz that the French alliance was not satisfactory and
that the Russian alliance might be far more productive. Had
Russia indeed become the cornerstone of Austria's alliance system the French alliance would quickly have dissolved and a
rapprochement with England might have developed, but Kaunitz,
unwilling to see such a drastic shift in "his system," dissuaded
Maria Theresa by arguing that reconciliation with England would
become essential. Disappointed as she was in the French, she
regarded any agreement with England as quite unpalatable.

Essentially the diplomatic history of the war was the story of
the unwinding of the French alliance and the binding of the
Habsburg interests to the Russian alliance—to the point that the
collapse of the alliance with St. Petersburg forced Maria Theresa

to make peace. Her hopes for France momentarily revived when Louis XV called Stainville home and appointed him foreign minister (December 3, 1758), having first rewarded him with the title Duke of Choiseul. This removed the most vocal advocate of a quick peace, Bernis, but Choiseul, though easier to negotiate with than his predecessor, was equally motivated by a conception of French interests rather than by any feeling of obligation to Habsburg interests. On the basis of this conception, he pressed for reexamination and redefinition of the alliance, a move that culminated in a new treaty (December, 1758). Maria Theresa was not unhappy with the new terms because, though reducing France's physical commitment, they did reaffirm that commitment, including support for Austrian reacquisition of Silesia. In one way, the new arrangement appeared to be more realistic and therefore more promising.

Reading the military history of the Seven Years' War leaves the peculiar impression that the Austrian war effort consisted largely of clever maneuvering which caused some minor discomfort to Frederick and produced jubilation in Vienna, jubilation invariably expressed by the performance of a *Te Deum* in St. Stephen's. What the Austrians failed to recognize was that their ally, Russia, was never able to follow up victories over Prussia (Zorndorff in 1758, Kay and Kunersdorf in 1759) because Austria never gave support. Frederick invariably regrouped his army and was never forced into a disorderly retreat. Maria Theresa, in her disillusionment with the French, correctly regarded the Russian alliance as the real key to a victory over Frederick, but failed to appreciate fully the necessity for the two allies to coordinate their efforts. This they never did, in part because Daun's whole conception of strategy ran counter to the requirements of such cooperation. Daun fought an essentially defensive war, shunning pitched battles, seeking to throw Frederick off balance, in effect to exhaust Frederick's resources by a war of movement. Thus in 1758 he had forced Frederick out of Bohemia with a brilliant series of marches and countermarches. In that way he avoided the gross tactical errors and subsequent defeats of his predecessor, Charles of Lorraine, and managed to limit Frederick's victory. But he also lost the advantage of obvious superiority in numbers which a combined allied offensive would have possessed. Worst of all, he did not seize the initiative in 1759 when Frederick himself, forced to abandon his offensive strategy, was convinced that the end was at hand.

Maria Theresa must share some of the blame. At best, Austria's war effort was always erratic. The reforms of 1749 had strengthened the state and the military organization, but the war placed too great a strain on the new order, forcing still further reforms. In addition, the Austrian generals with few exceptions were quite limited in their talents, and Maria Theresa's own interest and involvement in military matters only highlighted these limits. She saw more clearly than many of her generals the strategic demands created by the nature of the enemy, but her involvement in precise military decisions was both too great and too small. She interfered too much to allow the generals to feel free in their own determination of priorities. The unwillingness of the Austrian generals to act without reference to Maria Theresa was paralyzing, for it meant constant referral to Vienna. But, having conditioned her generals to hesitate to act without her approval, she was inconsistent in pressing them to make decisions. Maria Theresa was also overloyal to her generals. Having clung to Charles of Lorraine until his inadequacies could no longer be ignored, she then placed her trust too much in Daun. Even his failure to seize the offensive in 1759, when Frederick was on the verge of destruction, did not shake her confidence. Maria Theresa was not blind to Daun's faults, but she vigorously defended him against criticism. Thus, in 1760, when Choiseul denounced Daun for his unwillingness to fight a pitched battle, only Kaunitz's intervention deterred Maria Theresa from making an angry response that might well have broken relations between the two allies. If others knew better, she declared, why did they not give Daun more help.[6]

One of Maria Theresa's most decisive achievements was the selection of her advisers; one of her greatest weaknesses was her persistent loyalty to those who had served her well. She was not ruthless enough to discharge those whose service was no longer effective. She had demonstrated this humane flaw in her slowness to replace the tired and aging ministers of her father and she demonstrated it again with such men as Haugwitz and Daun. Leopold von Daun had already established himself in the military in Charles' reign, but it was Francis who first brought him to Maria Theresa's attention and he had participated in her coronation at Pressburg.[7] He served with some distinction

in the War of the Austrian Succession, displaying the organiza-
tional ability that would make him an important contributor to
the military reforms both before and after the Seven Years' War.
His experiences at the front during the first Silesian campaigns
also confirmed the basic strategy which he subsequently used
against Frederick. Daun later stated that he regarded as his
basic aim to avoid putting Maria Theresa in a position in which
she would be forced to make peace because she did not have a
battle-ready army. Daun moved into the inner circle of Maria
Theresa's friends in 1745 when he married Josefa, the older
daughter of the Countess Fuchs, who had been the queen's
"ayah" and who remained one of her closest confidants. Josefa
herself had been one of Maria Theresa's childhood intimates.
Subsequently the Dauns were regular guests in the royal household. Equally important were Daun's victories at Kolin and later
Hochkirchen (October 17, 1758). Maria Theresa found it hard
to condemn the author of those first delicious triumphs over the
hated Frederick.

By 1760 Choiseul adamantly declared that France could not
continue the war. Discouraged, Maria Theresa informed Starhemberg that for the sake of her friendship with France she
would work for peace, but her heart was not in it. To Kaunitz
fell entirely the task of making whatever gains were possible in
the circumstances. Austria's own need for peace was becoming
increasingly apparent. Despite minor successes in the campaign
of 1761, Maria Theresa recognized that Frederick was not yet
defeated, while her own resources were rapidly diminishing.
Furthermore the obvious decline of Tsarina Elizabeth meant the
Austro-Russian alliance was close to dissolution.

The Austro-Russian alliance ultimately depended on the anti-
Prussian sentiment of Elizabeth and her chancellor Bestuzhev.
With the fall of Bestuzhev in February, 1758, only the question-
able health of the dissolute tsarina protected the alliance that
Maria Theresa had once regarded as the mainstay of Austria's
hopes. The impending succession of the strongly pro-Prussian
Grand Duke Peter made such hopes chimerical. Kaunitz's grand
scheme in actuality was rather frail. Premised on the priority
of the Franco-Austrian agreement, his plan in the heat of battle
became more heavily dependent on Russia, clearly the most productive ally. Both facets of the alliance against Frederick were
weakened by the absence of any common base except an anti-

Prussian sentiment, which, however, was not equally intense with each of the partners. Their motives and aims were different and so no full trust was possible. Neither France nor Russia understood Austria's position and both pursued their own selfish ends, but Austria was equally oblivious to the needs of her allies. Perhaps Austria was the most remiss for, as the founder and leader of the coalition, she should have better comprehended the character of the allied cause.

Here too Maria Theresa must bear blame, for she viewed the war from a limited perspective. In a memorandum to the Austrian ambassador to Russia in 1757, Maria Theresa had declared that all European powers longed for peace so that they might devote themselves to the well-being of their peoples, but that Frederick had consistently thwarted this general desire. Always he sought means of extending his power, of preparing further attacks on his neighbors. Frederick's whole system, she asserted, was based on aggression and consequently there was little hope of change unless a new ruler with new hopes and principles should come to power in Prussia. She regarded Frederick as worse than a common criminal for the ill he could do was of such great magnitude, and she was convinced that so long as he ruled Prussia would remain a threat to the peace and stability of Austria and of Europe. She believed this passionately and argued it vehemently to her allies. Perhaps for that reason she could not understand that her allies did not share the fullness of her enmity, nor could she comprehend the complexities and subtleties of the conflict. She paid little heed to the great war for empire, though it influenced all France's decisions about the Continental war. She did have more understanding of Russia's position, though not necessarily evincing greater appreciation. Indeed Maria Theresa feared that Russia might acquire too much power in Eastern Europe and therefore opposed Russia's desire to annex East Prussia and part of Poland.

Her own last great effort in the struggle occurred after the campaign of 1759. With victory seemingly within reach, she plunged vigorously into the task of preparing the next campaign. Maria Theresa's readiness to involve herself in all aspects of the governance of her lands is nowhere more clearly evident than in the memoranda she prepared for the discussions of the War Council in the winter of 1759-1760 which range from concern for bullets and uniforms to the broadest questions of strategy.[8]

Maria Theresa overruled Daun's proposal in favor of one supported by Laudon and Kaunitz calling for a sweeping offensive in Silesia. When Laudon defeated Prussia at Landhut and captured Glatz and Breslau (June-July, 1760) Russia set her forces in motion. Daun, however, refused to commit his forces to a showdown with Frederick. Only after Maria Theresa intervened directly did he act, but by then it was too late. Frederick was able to entrench his forces and thus repulse Daun at Liegnitz (August 15, 1760). The Russians, disillusioned again by the irresolution of their ally, withdrew. The outcry against Daun was vociferous and Kaunitz urged Maria Theresa to give Laudon command, but Maria Theresa could not bring herself to degrade Daun. Instead she gave Laudon a hearty commendation and made him independent of Daun's command. In effect, Maria Theresa herself was assuming command. She immediately encouraged her generals to take energetic action, especially urging Daun to reestablish contact with the Russians. In October a combined Russian and Austrian force invested Berlin, but Frederick calmly attacked Daun in Saxony. The Battle of Torgau (November 3), among the bloodiest of the war, brought a brutal end to Maria Theresa's hopes.

Like Tsarina Elizabeth, the Austro-Russian alliance was dying. The court of Vienna watched helplessly as reports of her decline grew more frequent. The Russian military leaders, aware that with her death they would become Frederick's allies, lost all enthusiasm for the war. The campaign of 1761 was moribund, punctuated only by Laudon's energetic attempts to launch an offensive. On January 5, 1762, Elizabeth died. On February 23, Peter informed the Austrian ambassador that he was withdrawing from the war. The withdrawal was not actually accomplished until May 5 but Maria Theresa fully expected it to be followed by Russia's reentry on the side of Frederick—and it was. Ironically, Austria's best hope now appeared to depend on Daun's ability to outmaneuver the enemy, but Russian internal politics, not military events, proved to be Austria's salvation.

On July 9, 1762, Catherine overthrew her husband Peter and became the sole ruler of Russia. Maria Theresa wrote to her ambassador in Russia, "As long as we have lived there has been no news which has given us greater joy than the news of the fortunate accession of the Russian empress."[9] Saved from the disaster which Peter's short reign had threatened, Maria Theresa expected more from the upheaval in Russia than it in fact produced. Despite Catherine's strong dislike of Frederick, her own position would not permit her to reverse completely Peter's foreign policy; she contented herself by withdrawing from the war. Thus Maria Theresa's need for peace was little less urgent than before. Frederick also desired peace: his resources were depleted and he himself was exhausted. Russia's brief adherence to his cause had improved his position and thus he readily acceded to Maria Theresa's peace overtures. The Peace of Hubertusburg (February 15, 1763) was a victory for Frederick. Of the five alternate proposals for peace which Kaunitz had outlined in 1760, Austria in 1763 was forced to accept the least satisfactory: the *status quo ante bellum*. Maria Theresa again acknowledged the loss of Silesia and surrendered any attempt to gain compensation for the losses suffered on her behalf by her allies within the Empire. In return Frederick guaranteed the status of the Roman Catholic Church in Silesia and pledged his vote to Joseph in imperial elections.

The Diplomatic Revolution had not accomplished its initial aim, and both aspects of the alliance system, the tie with France and the one with Russia, had been found wanting. But Kaunitz, having constructed his system on the basis of his analysis of Austria's needs and her position in the world, could not envision the possibility that there was an inherent flaw in the system itself. Participation in the alliance might be imperfect, but that could be remedied. Thus in the dog days of 1760, when for all the successes of previous campaigns Austria's cause seemed no further advanced than it had been before the war, Kaunitz traced the problem to the faulty commitment of the individual allies. Cajolery and threats could improve French and Russian commitments, but Austria's failings derived from the weakness of her internal organization.

Complaints against the Haugwitzian system had never entirely ceased, but Maria Theresa managed to ignore them until the belated adherence of Kaunitz to the opposition brought the issue to a head.[10] Previously Kaunitz had shown little interest in internal affairs, devoting his whole interest to matters of diplomacy. His eventual intervention into domestic affairs had little to do with the theoretical question of centralized or decentralized power, nor was it the product of any desire on Kaunitz's part to assume leadership in internal as well as external affairs. He acted because the strain of the Seven Years' War on the still-emerging Haugwitzian state structure threatened to paralyze it and so to endanger the goals of his foreign policy. As early as August 6, 1758, and at the explicit request of Maria Theresa, Kaunitz ventured proposals to deal with the internal situation. Accepting centralization of power as a sound principle, he nonetheless argued that the Directory, though removing the disunifying effect of estate particularism, had introduced "departmental particularism" in its stead. To correct this defect, Kaunitz suggested the establishment of a State Council with powers of advisement and supervision and composed of the State Chancellor, the President of the War Council, and three or four other designated persons, who would not be heads of government departments, but would be of noble rank with special knowledge about certain areas of the Empire or certain departments.

Kaunitz had identified a significant weakness in the Directory, but there was no guarantee that his alternative would remedy it. In any case, it passed largely unnoticed until the military-diplomatic crisis of 1760. In November-December of 1760, Kaunitz presented to Maria Theresa a new version of the 1758 memorandum, now sharpened by his appraisal of the immediate dangers confronting Austria. Maria Theresa, convinced that Austria's situation was critical, readily accepted Kaunitz's proposal. There is, in fact, evidence to suggest that Kaunitz's intervention at this time was not made entirely on his own initiative, but that he had again, as in 1758, responded to a request from Maria Theresa, or possibly from the Emperor Francis. Kaunitz's proposal called for the establishment of the collegial principle in the government, as opposed to the notion of a prime ministry. Kaunitz rejected the latter idea, arguing on the one hand that the breadth and depth of knowledge which such a position would require could not be easily found in one man, and on the other that after all Maria Theresa was, in effect, her own prime minister. Even with the summoning of the Council on January 26, 1761, however, many observers believed that Kaunitz's special relationship with Maria Theresa made him prime minister in fact, though not in name.

Strikingly, the majority of the members of the State Council, including Haugwitz and Daun, although nominated by Kaunitz, were known to oppose his reforms. But his apparent magnanimity seems the less in light of the fact that when Haugwitz was named to the Council, an essentially advisory body, he was removed as chief of the Directory, the most important administrative organ in the government, and Daun's nomination to represent the War Council removed him from the field command.

The establishment of the Council did not involve a fundamental transformation of the existing system, but at the second meeting of the Council (January 30) he set forth his views on the basic principles of government and the battle lines were drawn. Maria Theresa herself quickly cut to the core of the real differences between Haugwitz and Kaunitz by responding with two questions: Should the separation of judicial and administrative functions be maintained? And should fiscal and political administration be divided? In posing the questions, Maria Theresa implied the possibility of making further reforms, but, not surprisingly, the majority of the Council supported Haugwitz who was particularly vehement in insisting on the combination of fiscal and political authority, the crux of his whole system. Maria Theresa hesitated, but the raising of the issue provoked all the opponents of Haugwitz's system to renew their criticisms. Kaunitz now asserted that the safety of the state required a decentralization of power, that is the separation of fiscal and political administration and the subdividing of fiscal authority. In December, 1761, by vote of the Council and with the full approval of the queen, the jurisdictions were separated.

In gaining his victory over Haugwitz, Kaunitz had had the support of those noblemen who had resisted the subjugation of the estates, but they erred in believing that the pre-1749 situation could be restored. Kaunitz himself was not in favor of a decentralization of power in the sense of weakening monarchial control. He was, like Maria Theresa, aristocratic in his viewpoint, but his aristocratic ideal was not that of the independent provincial nobility, but of the service nobility to which he himself belonged. Thus the principal result of Haugwitz's reforms, the advancement of state power, was equally the prime goal of the Kaunitzian system.[11] More accurately, Maria Theresa's initial and persistent purpose in sponsoring reform was the enhancement of royal power and any specific reform program had to comply with that intent.

Maria Theresa, who originally had championed the Haugwitzian system, lost faith in it under the influence of Kaunitz, but her faith was not transferred to the new system. She supported

Kaunitz while the war lasted, for she wanted to believe his argument that if internal affairs were set aright victory would be obtained, but her optimism dwindled and her doubts about Kaunitz's reform grew. Her doubts were well-founded for the flaws of the new system were soon obvious. Haugwitz's system had been imperfect, but it endured for twelve years until the weight of the war effort broke it down. Kaunitz's system, which was intended to strengthen Austria in face of the military burdens, endured for less than a third of that time: it could not bear the strain of peace.

As early as 1763, Maria Theresa indicated that a new solution to internal problems was required. Having laid the phantom of Silesia to rest, she had now to consolidate the great reforms of the past into a state system without the lost province. Haugwitz supplied the impetus for the new reforms. In early 1764 he sent Maria Theresa a detailed critique of Austrian administrative development since 1740. Therein he reiterated the basic principles which he had set forth in 1749, but he carefully indicated the errors in the structure built on those principles. Only by reasserting those principles and carrying them out more perfectly could the fiscal problems of the state be resolved. In the ensuing debate Kaunitz momentarily held back, but when no other defenders for the 1761 reform came forward he finally replied (May, 1764). The terms of his argument were almost identical to Haugwitz's: the principles of the system of 1761 were correct; it was the execution of those principles which had been faulty. Thus the battle was joined anew, and the Council was divided.

Maria Theresa recognized the need for change, but felt a strong affinity for Kaunitz's position. She called on Starhemberg to mediate the dispute, but to no avail. By the end of the year no progress had been made. In contrast to the firmness she had exhibited in the days of the first reforms, Maria Theresa seemed unable to commit herself to either faction or to the compromise she had asked Starhemberg to propose. Finally she presented to Kaunitz an anonymous proposal dated April 2, 1765, which while reiterating Kaunitz's argument that there was nothing fundamentally wrong with the system of 1761, insisted that the political and financial administrations, though separate, must work together. By endorsing this compromise Maria Theresa established it as the basic framework for the settlement. Discussions continued, but both Kaunitz and Haugwitz, realizing that only a final declaration on her part was necessary to resolve the matter, restricted their remarks to minor points and problems of implementation. Maria Theresa delayed, but apparently only because she wished to give Francis the opportunity to air his opinion. Given the opportunity in council, Francis, who had largely devoted his administrative activity to financial matters, supported without reserve his wife's position. On May 14, 1765, Maria Theresa gave her order for the last great administrative reform of her reign.

Kaunitz described the new reform as merely a completion of the basic organization established in 1761, but in fact there was a fundamental difference which led other observers to see the reform of 1765 as a return to Haugwitzian principles. The subdivision of the financial administration was replaced by a new centralization which was even more detrimental to the claims of the estates because it made the Exchequer the center of authority rather than the Court Chancellery. The Chancellery had been the constitutional organ through which the estates could assert their interests and thus they were more likely to influence fiscal decisions made there. With these decisions now made in the Exchequer, their powers of influence were diminished. There were still other indications of a renewed centralization, such as the submerging of the Commercial Council into the Court Chancellery. On the provincial level, agencies which the estates previously controlled were transformed into royal agencies. Only the continued distinction between financial and political jurisdiction detracted from the rapprochement with the Haugwitzian system. It remained to be seen what would become of the cooperation between the two jurisdictions which Maria Theresa had urged. Subsequent sessions of the State Council were concerned largely with the definition of the two jurisdictions, a task that was completed by an imperial order of August 26, 1765, in effect establishing a ministry of finance which was to proceed "in conjunction with the Chancellery."

Maria Theresa had fought her last war; she had made her last great administrative reform. A recent biographer has suggested that amidst the turmoil of the war Maria Theresa "began to rediscover her true nature."[12] In this view the determination with which Maria Theresa sought the reconquest of Silesia and the punishment of Frederick constituted an arrogance of power, which, if not alien to the queen's character, was nonetheless

nurtured, enticed and finally inflamed by the wiles of the serpen-
tine Kaunitz. "She would," the biographer notes, "have done
much better to stick to her original resolution and concentrate
on developing and consolidating the prosperity of her realm, leaving it to her successors, operating from strength, to find ways to
redress the wrong that had been done to her by Frederick."
But her original resolution had been nothing less than to exact
retribution; Kaunitz had merely offered her a means to gain an
end she thought both necessary and just. She had chosen Kaunitz
for that purpose, as she had chosen Haugwitz because he offered
her a way to strengthen the monarchy to make her task possible.
To have done less, to have left that responsibility to her heirs,
would have been a violation of trust. In later repenting for
"having made war out of pride," Maria Theresa did not reject a
mere aberration specifically identifiable with the Seven Years'
War, but the fundamental purpose of her policy for the first two
decades of her reign. In doing so she faulted part of her own
true nature. The "better nature" that eschewed war as an instrument of foreign policy and sorrowed over the agonies of
pursuing an active policy of domestic reform was but a part of
the real Maria Theresa. It was Maria Theresa growing old. The
aging process, however, was not only chronological; it was also
a product of a personal crisis that spanned the next decade.

CHAPTER VII

The Crisis of the Sixties

MARIA THERESA'S DESIRE' FOR PEACE ASSUAGED SOMEWHAT THE bitterness of defeat. Despite the many victories, despite the vastly improved showing of the army, despite the fortuitous escape from the catastrophe that threatened after Peter III's accession, Maria Theresa had not gained the objectives for which she had fought the war. But in peace perhaps she could enjoy the pleasures of family and friends which she had so frequently denied herself. Absence from family musical entertainments, hurried visits to the family circle, had been the hardest part of the price she paid for her steadfastness to duty.

Yet in the most anxious days she remained a continuing presence in the family. The elaborate instructions to tutors and the numerous letters she wrote to her children witness the constancy of her concern.[1] Even there, however, the inevitable duality of her role as mother and sovereign prevented her from being a completely private person. She could not then simply dote on her children, but had always to regard them critically, to view them politically as well as parentally. Illustrative of her attitude is this comment about her daughter Josefa:

Her facial traits are not attractive and her manner is likewise. She has something coarse about her. I would like my daughter not to be so self-willed. She is inclined that way. She is outwardly reserved and that is a good quality, especially in the country for which she is destined [she was betrothed to Ferdinand of Naples, the second son of the King of Spain], but it is not good to encourage this too much so that it will not have too great influence on her character and result in deception. It is better to encourage her to be kind and to have a cheerful disposition so that she finds means in herself, through work of all kinds, through reading, through painting and music and similar occupations, to entertain.[2]

Maria Theresa did not lose her concern for the right behavior of her children when they grew up. This concern is revealed time and again in the numerous letters she wrote after their departure from the family circle. In these missives expressions of maternal love and scraps of small talk mingle with a continuous stream of advice and counsel, sometimes in response to their requests, more often gratuitous, usually given gently, but not infrequently with the overtones of a scolding administered to a wayward child. Thus she counsels Joseph to treat others with charity and to accept their faults without scorn or irony; or she admonishes Ferdinand not to involve himself with persons of the theater.

The needs of public policy had great influence on the choice of mates for her children, though there was hardly anything extraordinary in this, given both Habsburg tradition and the practice of the times. More striking were the obvious evidences of Maria Theresa's genuine concern for the happiness of her children—though few attained it. The most graphic illustration of this concern involved Joseph. In October, 1760, Joseph married Isabella of Parma, a bride selected for him by Maria Theresa. Joseph had the happy—or unhappy—fortune to fall deeply in love with his young wife, but, after three years of marriage and the birth of one child, Isabella died (November 27, 1763). Joseph's grief and the grief which Maria Theresa shared with him are fully documented by the correspondence between them at this time. Joseph's sorrow was embittered by his awareness that almost immediately after Isabella's death efforts to find him a new wife had begun. Isabella had left a daughter, but a single child, especially a female child, was too thin a reed to support the interests of the dynasty. Maria Theresa, who understood the need of a second marriage for Joseph as clearly as anyone, nevertheless recognized that the matter must be treated delicately.

At first, Joseph was adamant in his assertions that it was unthinkable. His arguments were all based on his conviction that he could not find in a second marriage the same joy he had known in the first, but Maria Theresa patiently and lovingly argued in response the purely political need for the marriage. To this argument Joseph ultimately surrendered. At the same time, Maria Theresa sought a wife who would be agreeable to him, but when he expressed a preference it was for Louise of

Parma, the sister of his late wife, who was engaged to the Prince of Asturia. For the happiness of her son and her people, Maria Theresa wrote to the King of Spain to ask that the arrangement be broken so Joseph's wish might be gratified. However, as she had expected, the King of Spain would not agree and Kaunitz opposed exerting too much pressure for fear of straining the alliance with the Bourbons. Maria Theresa herself had first hoped that a marriage with Marie Louise of Spain could be arranged, but Joseph would not hear of it, and subsequently Marie Louise was married to Joseph's brother, Leopold. Other marital projects followed. A possible alliance with Portugal was vetoed for political reasons: it was thought unwise to bind the monarchy too closely to a state that on the one hand was over-dependent on England and on the other had strained relations with France. It was finally a political reason which determined the question in favor of a marriage with Maria Josepha of Bavaria: a marital tie with the Wittelsbachs promised to strengthen Austria's position in the Empire. On January 10, 1765, the wedding took place in Munich.

Maria Theresa wrote to her daughter Maria Christina:

You have a sister-in-law and I have a daughter-in-law: alas she is the princess Josepha. Against my conviction, against my heart, I have had to help my poor son make the decision which he could not declare alone or before the emperor and Kaunitz. Why had I to give the word which he would follow only for me. Imagine how that has made me feel. . . . The worst of it is that it is necessary to appear gay and contented . . . but my heart not being in accord with my reason, I have trouble composing myself. . . .[3]

Ironically, Joseph appeared more resigned than his mother; he wrote his brother later that while Josepha could never be his loving wife she would be a friend and welcome companion (though his subsequent behavior belied this sentiment). As it turned out, this marriage did not fulfill its political objective, for Josepha died of smallpox in 1767 without heir. Joseph refused to consider another marriage, but by then the pressure had decreased: his brother Leopold was safely married and in 1768 his wife produced an heir.

Apart from her family Maria Theresa found respite from the pressures of her duty in a small circle of friends. Court life in Theresian Austria was carried on in three circles.[4] The broadest

encompassed the general audiences to which innumerable people could come. As ceremonial occasions Maria Theresa's appearance at such levées was formal. The second circle was composed
of the queen's "greater" family and those men who held the
highest offices. Less formal than the first group, this still served
more as a symbolic assertion of the social status of the members than as a medium for social intimacies among them. It
did, however, function as an avenue for contact among the
politically important members of the government. The third and
narrowest circle was the intimate society of the royal pair and
entrance to it depended entirely on the will of Maria Theresa
or Francis.

While the manifestations of this relationship with the royal
couple were emphatically social (invitations to private suppers
at the Hofburg or Schönbrunn, or to holidays at Laxenburg)
there were also significant political implications. Daun and
Haugwitz, for example, both had ready access to the queen
and also developed a close personal relationship with each
other which influenced their actions in the State Council. Maria
Theresa's fondness for them and their families gave them a
certain security, but it did not guarantee them political preeminence. They—as well as Bartenstein who if not a member
of the inner circle was still an intimate of the queen—could not
retain Maria Theresa's political support when they came into
conflict with Kaunitz. That singular man, who by his very nature
held himself aloof from all social intimacies, remained her most
trusted adviser, though never her friend in the same sense as
Daun or Haugwitz. It is a further demonstration of Maria
Theresa's political aptitude that while she honored personal
loyalties she did not allow them to blind her.

Since the Treaty of Aix-la-Chapelle (1748), Austria had made
efforts to elect Joseph as King of the Romans and thus to guarantee Habsburg succession to the imperium. Frederick had consistently opposed the election, while the other electors sought
extensive concessions from the Habsburgs in terms of subsidies,
religious guarantees, extensions of princely prerogatives, and
new limitations on the imperial power. Though willing to grant
subsidies, Maria Theresa regarded the other demands as excessive. Still, she had persevered, though with little hope of success.
The Peace of Hubertusburg (1763), however, reopened the
question in earnest as a result of the treaty article in which

Frederick pledged his vote to Joseph.[5] Within a month of the peace settlement, Kaunitz had convinced Maria Theresa to press for the election, and negotiations with the various electors were undertaken. Kaunitz saw the election not only as a guarantee of the dynasty's claim to the imperium, but as a means of attaining closer ties with certain of the German states, and he was not willing to allow this opportunity to be lost. His negotiations were successful and on March 27, 1764, Joseph was elected King of the Romans.

The wisdom of acquiring the Roman kingship and indeed of pressing for Joseph's remarriage (the failure of his second marriage to provide dynastic continuity could not have been foreseen) received disheartening confirmation in 1765. In August of that year the family journeyed to Innsbruck for the marriage of Archduke Leopold and Marie Louise of Spain. Following the nuptials, the family had remained there. While attending the palace theater on the evening of August 18, Francis felt some discomfort and so left the performance early. Traversing the corridor connecting the theater and the palace, he staggered. Joseph, who had followed him, rushed to his aid, but Francis waved him away. The emperor took several more steps, then collapsed into his son's arms. Carried to a nearby side-chamber, he died without regaining consciousness. Maria Theresa, herself indisposed, had not gone to the theater, but now hearing the bustle of activity, hurried to the scene. Speechless, tearless, she fell to her knees beside her husband's body. Finally she was led back to her apartments. The next day she had her hair cut short and ever after wore mourning.

To her son Ferdinand she wrote:

One can bear the misfortune to which he would otherwise succumb only by resigning oneself to the will of God; there is no other consolation. You have lost the best and most affectionate father, the subjects the greatest prince and gracious father, and I have lost everything, a loving husband, a perfect friend, who was my only support and to whom I owed everything.[6]

A year later she complained, "Here again is that unhappy month the name of which I cannot hear, speak or write without shuddering."[7] On a scrap of paper discovered in her prayer book after her death, she had carefully reckoned the time, down to the hours (258,744) of her married life.[8] In later years she berated herself for having made too little of those precious hours: "All my hours are full of thoughts of my vanished happiness, not without bitter regret that while he was with me I did not make enough of it."[9]

The constant demands of government had been the greatest thief of time, and the exalted conception which Maria Theresa held for her responsibility prevented her from fully sharing the experience of power with Francis. Undoubtedly he had assumed that far greater authority would devolve to him and was frustrated when it did not. Even when eagerly she sought his counsel (and there was a genuineness in her need for his presence) he remained always aware that she retained for herself the power of decision. In that fact rests the strange dichotomy of her rule.

For consolation Francis had turned to other pursuits. His passion for hunting was maintained. Maria Theresa in educating her sons warned: "Hunting is nothing more than a sport; it is not a profession."[10] He was less loving than she, and clearly not so faithful, not being averse to pursuing fairer game. The reports of foreign ambassadors make note of his flirtations and in 1755 he established the liaison with Princess Auersperg. In a letter to her daughter Maria Amalia who complained of the infidelities of her husband, Ferdinand of Parma, Maria Theresa wrote:

The more you reveal your feelings and your trust in leaving your husband free, the more devoted he will be. All happiness consists of trust and constant kindness. Foolish love is soon past, but you must respect each other, and wherever possible be useful to each other. Each must prove the other's true friend, in order to be able to bear the misfortunes of life and to establish the welfare of the House. . . .[11]

But Francis was not a mere court decoration—though he often gave that impression. During his limited stay in Florence he had demonstrated administrative skills. Subsequently, these skills were directed almost entirely to the monarchy's economic policies and even more particularly to the organization of the family's personal estates and wealth. To be sure, he had limited influence on the great matters of state. As Maria Theresa herself seemed to weaken in resolution in the early 1760's, however, Francis had an opportunity to assume a more prominent role, but his sudden death extinguished the possibility. In any case, having reigned for twenty-five years while his wife ruled, Francis may no longer have possessed the will to use the opportunity.

Of necessity the co-regency with Joseph was a partnership of a different quality than the co-regency with Francis. Though she held a deep affection for her son, she could not bring him into her confidence as she had Francis, nor was it possible for him to accept the role as adviser rather than co-ruler as Francis had done. Having regarded many of his father's activities as frivolous, Joseph was determined to live a more useful existence. Conversely, the importance Maria Theresa attached to Joseph's education did not mean that she was necessarily any readier to concede effective authority to the new co-regent. In fact Maria Theresa pressed for the co-regency for Joseph for much the same reason as she had for Francis: imperial politics.[12] As Maria Theresa's legal heir and possessor of the Roman kingship, Joseph's claim to the imperium was indisputable, but like Francis, Joseph had no real territorial power base—in this respect he was even weaker than Francis because his father had held Tuscany. The alternative was to create a separate holding for Joseph, but Maria Theresa opposed such an alienation of dynastic lands. To be sure Maria Theresa desired some help from her son in a moment when the depression of bereavement had led her to contemplate abdication. She spoke of retreating to a convent to spend her days in quiet grief, but the inexorable sense of duty which had estranged her from the life she would have preferred as wife and mother would not now permit her to indulge in the melancholy pleasure of widowhood. God had so ordained her life that she must rule: for that reason she did not abdicate, nor could she defer authority to Joseph.

To the extent that Joseph could subordinate himself to her authority, he could function as her minister, as an agent of the queen; to the extent that his youth and aggressiveness impelled him to lead, he would clash with her. Mutual love and esteem and an informal division of jurisdiction kept the co-regency from dissolution. In effect, Maria Theresa retained control over internal affairs while Joseph assumed increasing authority in foreign affairs. (More strictly Maria Theresa accorded Joseph jurisdiction over the army and military reorganization.) The division of responsibility was tentative and quite imperfect: on the one hand, the omnipresent Kaunitz complicated the problem of authority and, on the other, neither Maria Theresa nor Joseph restricted the scope of their activities.

The death of Francis and the beginning of the co-regency with Joseph mark what biographers have traditionally viewed as a distinct break in Maria Theresa's life and many have regarded the period 1765-1780 as a mere appendage to her reign. That a perceptible shift in her reign occurred is undeniable and the loss of her husband and the accession of her son contributed significantly to the shift; but they also form part of a series of events that befell Maria Theresa in this period and which, taken together, provide the explanation for the change.

The Seven Years' War profoundly affected Maria Theresa. Her own urgent desires to right a past wrong, to punish the evildoer and restore a lost jewel to her crown, had helped to cause the war. The momentous efforts at reform had been directed toward making fulfillment of those desires possible and in 1759-1760 they had seemed so close to attainment. But victory eluded her and catastrophic defeat had hovered dangerously near. The failure to regain Silesia, Austria's inability to take advantage of her opportunities, the changes of fortune that broke the great alliance which was to have punished the iniquitous Frederick: all these things dulled her spirit and caused her to grow old.

The increasing frequency of depressions and of irresolution from the late 1750's may have resulted from the feminine "change of life." In any case there are clear evidences of physiological alterations. Already broadened by sixteen pregnancies, Maria Theresa became more and more corpulent—after the death of Francis she let herself go to the point she could sleep comfortably only in a sitting position. She seemed perpetually overheated and developed a passion for fresh air and lemonade: she insisted on full ventilation in all rooms whatever the weather, and would conduct business seated by an open window, fanning herself and sipping from an omnipresent glass. This physical eccentricity may have begun earlier in her life but it intensified with the "hot flashes" characteristic of menopause, persisting through the rest of her life.

The death of Francis was not the only personal loss she suffered. Three of her sixteen children had died in infancy, but in the 1760's she lost three more. Karl Joseph had died in 1761 and Johanna in 1762. At the very time Francis died, Leopold, newly married to Marie Louise of Spain, was ailing and Maria

Theresa feared for his life. Though he recovered, Josepha, who had succeeded Johanna as the betrothed of Ferdinand of Naples, followed her to the grave (1767). Maria Theresa herself fell seriously ill with the smallpox and few expected her to recover. She bore the scars for the rest of her life as did her daughter Maria Elizabeth, who thus lost her prospects for marriage and would live out her days in bitterness at the court. Maria Theresa had also been deeply affected by the death in 1763 of Isabella of Parma, Joseph's young and beautiful wife. The day before Isabella's death Maria Theresa wrote to Kaunitz: "We are approaching the tragic death of an angel; I do not believe she will live out the night. All my joy, all my peace die with this delightful and incomparable daughter, for whom I thank God."[13] She similarly felt the grief of her son when the only child of his marriage to Isabella, Maria Theresa, died in 1770.

To the deaths in the family were added those of two of Maria Theresa's closest and most trusted advisers, Haugwitz (September, 1765) and Daun (February, 1766). To Haugwitz's widow, Maria Theresa confided that she had lost a "great minister and a true friend." Daun's death followed that of his wife, one of the queen's childhood playmates and a valued companion in maturity. Following the demise of the husband, Maria Theresa wrote:

> God has taken from me the two persons who rightly possessed all my trust. Both were pious Christians and were filled with zeal and devotion, both spoke truthfully to me and to both I could open my heart without hesitation. Now I am deprived of that source of help.[14]

To this dismal chronicle of lost friends one must add the deaths of Bartenstein in 1767, Sylva-Tarouca in 1771, and Van Swieten in 1772.

There would be no more grand projects to reform the state, no more campaigns to restore the lost provinces. Gone were the energy and the enthusiasm with which she had supported Haugwitz in his efforts to establish a strong and efficient central government, the determination with which she had approved and abetted the diplomatic ventures of Kaunitz. She did not retreat to a nunnery as she had threatened but in a way she brought the nunnery to court. The colorful family circle captured by the court painter Martin van Meytens dwindled and the baroque blues and reds and golds were replaced by the constant somberness of mourning. The intoning of mass and the querulous complaints of her maiden daughters, Maria Anna and Maria Elizabeth, both titular abbesses of religious orders, became the sounds of court. In the young and beautiful queen, the virtues were magnificent, the faults viewed with tolerance. The somberness, the weariness of the monarch dulled the virtues, darkened the faults, and wearied the people.

The supreme irony of her reign had yet to be unfolded: the peculiar alliance of purpose between herself and her archfoe Frederick of Prussia. The vivid contrast between these two German monarchs had found an epic manifestation in the conflict that flamed between them from the moment of their nearly simultaneous accessions to power. To Frederick, Maria Theresa became the archetype of the malevolent, irrational she-ruler, the creator and preserver of the feminine conspiracy that surrounded and harassed him. He is said to have referred to her unkindly as "the great milch-cow of Europe," thus expressing a thinly veiled disgust at her fertility. Not surprisingly, after the Battle of Mollwitz (April 10, 1741), he selected as the proper text for the service of thanksgiving Paul's admonition: "Let the women learn in silence with all subjection. But I suffer not a woman to teach, nor to usurp authority over the man, but to be in silence" (I Timothy 2:11-12). Maria Theresa returned the sentiment. To her, Frederick was a beast, a barbarian, a vain and deceitful despot without faith, without morality, without law. It is too much to suppose that these vigorous antipathies were ever fully dissipated, yet they too became exhausted by the strains of war and diluted by the desire for peace.

Subsequently she berated Frederick for his hand in forcing her to act against her will in the Polish crisis, but she did come to recognize that in her struggle to keep the peace he was her best ally, and he in turn recognized her achievements as head of the House of Habsburg. They never met. There is an allegorical depiction of them exchanging an olive branch after the Peace of Hubertusburg: broad-beamed baroque angels hover in the background, one trumpeting, one carelessly holding a laurel wreath over Frederick's head; in the foreground crouches an anguished mother clutching her infants; Frederick, erect and elegant, extends the olive branch, his eyes expectant; Maria Theresa, regal, maturely beautiful, is reaching to receive the token, but her eyes are averted, looking absently beyond the viewer, into space, into time.

It was Frederick who said after the war: "What concerns me, poor old man that I am, is that I return to a city which I recognize only by its walls, where I perceive no one of my old acquaintances. . . ."[15] The words were Frederick's, the tone of weariness, of estrangement, he shared with his great rival.

Power remained, but she no longer exercised it so firmly. The reforms of 1764-1765 mark Maria Theresa's last effort to effect a fundamental change in the system. Subsequent reforms and alterations aimed at increasing efficiency, but the system itself was not changed, or questioned—at least by Maria Theresa. The purpose of her reforms from the beginning, after all, had been to conserve and strengthen the monarchy, not to utterly transform it. Now the process of conserving had to her become a more passive task. She may also have come to question the real efficacy of administrative reforms. The reforms she did press had less to do with the functioning of the state apparatus than with fulfilling what she regarded as her obligation to the people. To be sure there was a new voice to be heard, the young, vigorous though not yet fully articulate voice of Joseph, but Maria Theresa's own became hesitant, vacillating. Increasingly, she seemed to defer decisions to Joseph or to Kaunitz—yet to neither did she concede the authority to sustain them.

CHAPTER VIII

The Co-regency with Joseph: Domestic Affairs

THE LAST FIFTEEN YEARS OF MARIA THERESA'S REIGN, THE TIME of the co-regency with Joseph, were rife with tension and frustration: a stubborn sense of duty struggled with an aggressive will to power; a world view pervaded by the baroque competed with the newer spirit of the Enlightenment; a mother tried both to control and to conciliate her son. They loved, respected, but finally did not understand each other, and so they quarreled. The quarrels were complicated by the omnipresent Kaunitz, who was both a bridge and a barrier between the two. A review of domestic affairs after 1765 suggests the troika as an apt symbol of the relationship among Maria Theresa, Joseph, and Kaunitz—but it is apt only if one recalls that, however many the horses, there remained one driver. Maria Theresa occasionally lost control of the machine, particularly if Joseph and Kaunitz pulled together, but neither co-regent nor minister could sustain effective control himself.

Theresian reform was essentially pragmatic, concerned with specific issues, because Maria Theresa, who ultimately determined the fate of all reforms, did not share the philosophy which could provide ideological justification for them. Though she had never read the *philosophes,* she had firm opinions about them, regarding their ideas as impoverished, rooted entirely in moral egotism, and thus without the deep sources which might sustain them. To her youngest son Maximilian she wrote that she might comprehend, though she could not accept, those ideas if their proponents were more fortunate in their enterprises and more satisfied in their personal lives than other men, but observation proved the contrary. She both rebuked the *philosophes* and regarded them as dangerous, for "They condemn the entire past

because of its ignorance and prejudices without knowing anything about the past and little more about the present."[1] On
several occasions during the trying days of the co-regency, when
her own resolution failed her and Joseph's eagerness to rule
overwhelmed her, she considered abdication, but invariably
rejected the idea. Not love of power, but the haunting fear that
the principles of her heir were unwise, restrained her. Thus in
December, 1775, when relations between them reached their
nadir, Maria Theresa tersely and angrily informed Joseph, "I am
too old ever to accommodate myself to such principles, but I
wish and pray to God that my successor will never put them to
the test. Neither he, nor even less his successors, will be the
happier."[2] Specifically, she condemned Joseph's support for religious freedom, his attacks on noble rights, and his advocacy
of greater social and economic freedom.

Relatively early in her reign Maria Theresa had declared:

> From the outset I decided and made it my principle, for my own
> inner guidance, to apply myself, with a pure mind and instant prayer
> to God, to put aside all secondary considerations, arrogance, ambition,
> or other passions, having on many occasions examined myself in
> respect of these things, and to undertake the business of government
> incumbent on me quietly and resolutely—a principle that has, indeed,
> been the one guidance which saved me, with God's help, in my
> great need, and made me follow the resolution taken by me, making
> it my chief maxim in all I did and left undone to trust only in God,
> Whose almighty hand singled me out for this position without move
> or desire of my own and Who would therefore also make me worthy
> through my conduct, principles, and intentions to fulfill properly the
> tasks laid on me, and thus to call down and preserve His almighty
> protection for myself and those He has set under me, which truth
> I held daily before my eyes and maturely considered that my duty
> was not to myself but only to the public.[3]

She thus summarized the central assumptions of her politics: the
absolute conviction that God had called her to rule and the
equally firm belief that she ruled for the benefit of her people.
For her, the latter derived from the former. The divine action
which enthroned her was explicitly a commission to care for
those whom God had set under her, not a sign of God's special
favor for her or her family. She—indeed her dynasty—was not
called because she was worthy, but God would make her worthy
to fulfill His purposes in calling her. Thus she regarded the state

as a Christian commonwealth and felt morally impelled to defend the religion of the land. More especially she had a religious obligation "to safeguard the true faith and the souls of her subjects."[4] Her overpowering sense of religious obligation was fundamental to all her reforms.

Given this sense she viewed full religious toleration as an unthinkable policy for any Catholic ruler. To her, religious toleration was virtually synonymous with indifferentism: how could one rule in the name of God if one had so little love for His truth that one allowed everyone to pursue his own fantasies? She admonished Joseph: "Such talk from you can cause the greatest calamity and make you answerable for many thousands of souls."[5] Still convinced of the validity of the formula "One faith, one law, one king," Maria Theresa also concluded that religious toleration invited political disorder: "What would become of us without an established cult, without submission to the Church? Peace and contentment could not endure; the rule of force and other unhappy consequences would follow, as one has already seen. [She referred to disturbances in Bohemia in 1775.]."[6]

As a result of the unrest in Bohemia Maria Theresa resolved to expunge Protestantism from her lands to save the monarchy and the souls of her subjects. Joseph responded vigorously to her proposal, arguing that in trying to save souls, Maria Theresa would only destroy bodies, and that religious belief should not be forced. When Kaunitz supported Joseph and Joseph threatened to abdicate (1777), Maria Theresa conceded. Kaunitz himself was little concerned with the question of freedom of conscience, but he argued that religious uniformity could not be enforced and any attempt to do so would only induce further unrest.

That Maria Theresa conceived the monarch as a keeper of souls and believed religious unity was a requisite of political order constituted the crucial difference between her view and Joseph's, and this difference necessarily appeared most vividly in the issue of toleration. Other aspects of their religious policies, however, demonstrated an essential continuity. The religious reforms of the Josephian decade (1780-1790) were indeed not substantially different from those of the period 1748-1780. Rather the uniqueness and significance of Josephinism resides in the fact that Joseph proceeded in a different spirit.[7]

The essential flavor of Theresian religious policy is manifest in the measures themselves: restrictions on the number and wealth of convents; abolition of the right of asylum; limitation of the powers of ecclesiastical courts; establishment of royal approval as the prerequisite for publication of papal bulls and decrees within the monarchy. In spirit and intent these measures were one with Maria Theresa's administrative and fiscal reforms, thus with the process of rationalizing and consolidating royal power. For Joseph, for Kaunitz, for other advisers on religious questions (including Francis prior to his death) the motivation was more diverse, and frequently more ideological, but their influence on religious policy depended on their ability to justify their proposals to Maria Theresa in her terms. Because of the ideological predilections of Kaunitz and others, they might read more into the reforms than Maria Theresa intended, but in turn they were checked by her intentions.

In his own day Kaunitz enjoyed the reputation of being a profound thinker and subsequently some historians have regarded him as the "philosopher of Josephinism," but his ideas on the religious question were little more than a mélange of *étatisme*, Gallicanism, and basic social contract theory.[8] Nevertheless Kaunitz's essentially political view of the question was far more likely to appeal to Maria Theresa than was a more blatantly philosophical view. Kaunitz was also clever enough to cater to the religious sensitivities of Maria Theresa. Kaunitz was undeniably anticlerical and frequently betrayed this bent in his behavior toward the clergy; he may also have been a freethinker, but he invariably justified his proposals for religious reforms on the basis of reasons of state and he seldom allowed his personal disdain for the clergy to interfere with political or diplomatic advantage. Thus he regularly cautioned that the Papacy was an important foreign power and should not be indiscriminately assailed; thus also he rejected some of the more radical proposals for asserting state control over the Church in favor of policies which provided the reality of such control but retained an appearance acceptable to the Church. (For example, he advocated secular control over episcopal nominations by the judicious exercise of a veto over unacceptable papal appointments rather than having the state assume the power of appointment.)

Kaunitz was also involved in the Jesuit question, as was Van

Swieten. The expulsion of the Jesuits emphasized that the Gallican idea provided the basis for the religious policy of the co-regency: political, not philosophical, issues were paramount. As early as 1749 Van Swieten had pressed for the exclusion of the Jesuits from the censorship commission and he had persuaded Maria Theresa to eliminate their control of the theological faculty at the University of Vienna. When the clamor against the Jesuits in the rest of Europe reached a peak in 1768, Kaunitz, then Van Swieten, urged her to expel them from the monarchy. Maria Theresa hesitated to join the attack, and the Jesuits themselves looked to her for protection. Surrounded by advisers who pressed for the abolition of the order, and determined to maintain good relations with the Bourbons who led the anti-Jesuit campaign, Maria Theresa finally acquiesced. By 1773 the suppression of the Jesuits was a virtual reality. Maria Theresa at that point intervened, not to preserve the Order, but to obtain a guarantee that the state rather than the Papacy would receive the confiscated property. This condition accepted, the abolition was carried out. The members of the Society were treated liberally in Austria, with a portion of their forfeited wealth being used to distribute pensions; the remainder was used to assist some of the queen's favorite educational reforms.

How could Maria Theresa, a pious daughter of the Church, favor policies that undeniably restricted the power of the Church in her dominions? Ferdinand Maass asserted that her policies and her piety were not compatible, that she permitted the enactment of measures injurious to the Church perhaps without being aware of the consequences. In contrast, Friedrich Walter argued that Maria Theresa's piety and policy were quite compatible, that indeed the Church itself recognized the necessity for and efficacy of the policies she pursued.[9] In fact, for Maria Theresa, *raison d'état* resolved the dilemma and no conflict of purpose existed. Spanagel's lessons on the Investiture Controversy found an echo in the advice which Maria Theresa tendered Leopold as he prepared to assume his responsibilities as Grand Duke of Tuscany (1765), advice which aptly summarizes her own policy: "Prove yourself a good Son to the Holy Father in all matters of religion and dogma. But be sovereign, and do not permit the Roman court to meddle in governmental affairs."[10]

Maria Theresa's fervent adherence to royal sovereignty provided the context for her criticism of Joseph's disdain for noble rights. No quiescent believer in the virtues of the nobility, she had long recognized particularly the provincial nobility with its power rooted in the historic estates as the principal obstruction to the advance of royal power. From the beginning her reform program had aimed at eliminating that obstructive use of power. Despite her concerted attack on the estates, however, Maria Theresa did not deny, nor did she wish to subvert, the nobility's special status in society. Rather she sought to delineate and defend its true and proper place. She had acknowledged noble privileges in her various coronation oaths, but "Since the formula of confirmation speaks expressly of 'honorable, ancient customs,' the maintenance of them is rightly to be understood as only applying to those ancient customs which are good, not to the bad."[11] The feeling that she had accomplished this task restrained Maria Theresa from pressing further political reforms after 1765. Concerned to assert the sovereignty of the crown, she nevertheless recognized limits on that sovereignty. She feared that Joseph, unmindful of those limits, would disrupt society by his rash assertions of royal prerogatives.

Maria Theresa's treatment of the Hungarian nobility provides a particularly striking example of her policy. The most independent of Maria Theresa's dominions, Hungary had received confirmation of its status through the agreement by which the Hungarian Estates had accepted the Pragmatic Sanction and again through Maria Theresa's coronation oath, yet their acceptance of the Sanction also acknowledged Hungary's place as part of a greater whole. Maria Theresa steadfastly sought to bind her ever closer to the *Gesammtmonarchie*. She did this by the proverbial carrot-and-stick method. On the one hand, she heaped honors on the Hungarian nobility, founding the Hungarian Royal Bodyguard and the Order of St. Stephen (both in 1765) and providing generous loans to impecunious Hungarian nobles. She also offered preferment in the army and civil service to sons, helped to arrange advantageous marriages for sons and daughters, and bestowed honored places in religious orders on unmarried daughters. Alternatively, she attempted to denationalize the nobility by granting lands and titles in Hungary to non-Magyars. Even as she pursued the policy of friendly persuasion she found it necessary to tighten her grip. In 1764-1765 the apparent ingratitude of both the Diet and the Count Palatine, Lajos Batthyány, only recently made a prince of the Holy Roman

Empire, induced Maria Theresa to abandon her attempt to work with the Diet, and thereafter she governed Hungary by extraordinary measures. The Diet, previously in abeyance since 1751, did not meet again during her reign and the office of Count Palatine remained vacant after Batthyány's death (1765). Instead, she guided Hungarian affairs through a lieutenant-governor of her own choosing. Maria Theresa's extraconstitutional procedure had more symbolic meaning than actual political consequences for the powers of the Count Palatine were minimal and even the Diet was not vital to the survival of the Hungarian monarchy's unique status. In the years ahead, however, and especially after 1780, the symbol took on added significance. Maria Theresa's urbarial patent of 1767, by which she sought to standardize serf obligations throughout Hungary, made it clear that she did not intend Hungary to lead an existence entirely separate from her other lands. Her reluctance to impose on Hungary certain administrative reforms introduced elsewhere reflects her strategy and not her goals. Joseph's ultimate failure, then, resulted not from an attempt to reverse her policy but from trying to carry it too far and too fast.

The urbarial patent also provides another insight into her attitude toward the nobility. Through this action Maria Theresa hoped to increase state control over the peasants, to improve their ability to pay taxes, and to guarantee them greater justice. For her the last was not the least of her concerns and in emphasizing it she declared: "I must serve justice to rich and poor alike. I must answer my conscience. I do not want to be damned for the sake of a few magnates and noblemen."[12]

The issue of administrative reform particularly vexed Maria Theresa because Joseph and Kaunitz sharply disagreed on it and so it constantly threatened to dissolve the triumvirate. Joseph had hardly become co-regent before he dispatched a long memorandum to his mother calling for a reform of the administrative system, specifically proposing to transform the State Council into a cabinet headed by a prime minister. Kaunitz successfully rebuffed this effort, in part because with the deaths of Francis and Haugwitz Maria Theresa felt unable to dispute the wisdom of her chancellor. Criticism of the system persisted, however, and with good reason: by 1770 the Council had almost ceased to function—three of its eight members were out of the country, a fourth was incapacitated by illness, and Kaunitz had received permission to absent himself from discussions of internal affairs. Not surprisingly, in the spring of 1771 Joseph reopened his campaign for reform, arguing with urgency that if the monarchy were to avoid disaster, leadership had to be vested in a single omnicompetent individual, presumably himself. Maria Theresa had already considered the feasibility of consolidating certain offices and had even requested Count Hatzfeld to provide her with a proposal to that end. Hatzfeld's memorandum was similar in many ways to Joseph's proposal and was based on the reunification of financial and political authority, thus on the principles of Haugwitz. Despite his efforts to avoid formal responsibility for directing internal affairs, Kaunitz had not abandoned his interest in them and his opposition prevented an actual constitutional change, although Hatzfeld was able to effect a coordination of the political and financial authority by virtue of the offices which he held, Court Chancellor and Director of the State Council. Though acknowledging that such a consolidation was desirable, Maria Theresa relieved Hatzfeld of some of his functions in December, 1771, and thereby disrupted the personal centralization of authority he had effected.

In 1772, Joseph again submitted a proposal for reform, but once more he failed to transfer his own sense of urgency to his mother. Joseph's eagerness finally stimulated Kaunitz to prepare a long memorandum concerning the internal organization of the state, which, however, Joseph dismissed as a tissue of impractical theoretical ideas. This rebuff provoked Kaunitz to offer his resignation (December, 1773). Maria Theresa refused to accept it, saying

> Let us see whether there is still a way after thirty-three years of laborious and faithful service, that we might together accomplish something to save the State. If there is no such way, then let us retire together, but not otherwise. . . .[13]

Kaunitz had no sooner acceded to her wishes than Joseph declared that he would abdicate. Joseph complained that while he knew the administrative structure was faulty, he was not permitted to do anything about it, while Maria Theresa on her part seemed unable or unwilling to act. In letters to his brother Leopold at this time Joseph reiterated time and again his conviction that the state was paralyzed.

Maria Theresa's response was in part a declaration of despair, an admission of the very inability to act which so distressed her son, but it was also an admonition that he had failed to give her the help she required. She said she was willing to hand over all power to him, but that he himself had repeatedly rejected this alternative:

> Since you are not prepared to give commands yourself; then I must confess to you if you intend to give me support in confronting this great task before me that my mind and my ability, my sight, my hearing, my quickness of thought, are all failing me and that the fault which I have feared all my life, indecision, is increasing as my courage fails me and I am deprived of those whom I trust. . . . Tell me what you wish me to do; nothing will be too great a sacrifice to relieve me from the miserable situation in which I have lived for the last six years.[14]

There followed a reconciliation between Joseph and Kaunitz by which the latter was assured that Joseph shared Maria Theresa's esteem for him, but the matter of reforming the State Council still hung fire. Maria Theresa had decided to turn the whole problem over to Joseph. Kaunitz continued to oppose the appointment of a minister-in-chief on the grounds that that would make of the Council something other than it was intended to be. Now Maria Theresa pressed Joseph to resolve the question. By a decree of May 12, 1774, the Council received certain characteristics of the old Directory and thereafter Maria Theresa was wont to call Kaunitz the head of the State Council, but in actuality the Council remained an advisory body and not a cabinet or collegial authority. No further attempts to alter the Council were made during Maria Theresa's lifetime.

The dispute over the State Council was the central problem of political-administrative history during the co-regency. The positions taken on this question by the three principal protagonists were indicative of their basic views of state organization at this point: Joseph was and would continue to be the advocate of a federal state and thus of a centralized and clearly hierarchic administration. Kaunitz, a fervent supporter of dynastic power and an opponent of the power of the estates, was nevertheless a member of the nobility and therefore anxious to uphold the privileges of that group, which he saw as the chief support of the monarchy. Centralization in the Haugwitzian and now Josephian sense he saw as destructive of the proper relationship between monarchy and the state, for all authority should be centered in the ruler, not in a bureaucratic apparatus which would limit the monarchy on the one hand and encroach on the privileges of the nobility on the other. Maria Theresa clearly inclined toward Kaunitz's position, yet her primary concern was to keep both her son and her long-time servant at her side. Her actions in this crisis were a paradigm of her behavior for the rest of her reign: grieved by the tensions and disputes which marred the relationship with Joseph, she often thought of abdicating, handing over all power to her beloved son who seemed so anxious for the authority she now regarded as a crushing burden; but, dedicated to the welfare of her people, convinced that she ruled by God's will, she clung to power because she doubted the wisdom of her son's ideas.

You move too quickly in your thought. That is all very well for a private person, but for him who governs it is better to reflect and to hold to the maxims and statutes of the land and to follow them; and he ought to turn away from them only if he can improve on them, not just by his own testimony, but by the testimony of others. We are accountable to no one except Him who has given us this place in order to govern according to His holy law the people whom we should love and protect against all.[15]

Here again emerges the sense of religious obligation which was the deepest motive of Maria Theresa's reign. It explains her persistent concern for the people. It enabled her to conceive quite radical solutions to the problems of the peasant at the very time she criticized Joseph for his dangerous advocacy of greater social and economic freedom. Confronted by the widespread peasant unrest of 1774-1775 following on the Bohemian famine of 1770-1772, Maria Theresa admonished her son for his loose talk, bemoaned her weakness and frailty, and wearily debated with herself whether she should abdicate.[16] But reminded that a higher will than her own had bestowed on her the reins of power, Maria Theresa turned away from the compelling idea of abdication. Restrengthened, she confronted the problem with the conviction that merely quelling the disturbances in the countryside was not sufficient, that a fundamental reform in the organization of rural society was necessary.

In this instance, Maria Theresa approached the question of manorial services cautiously, for it was bound to provoke antagonism. Caution meant vacillation since the conflict of interests was too great to permit a compromise and Maria Theresa feared to offend. Only the firmness of her belief that something more than suppression was necessary kept the question open. Joseph desired a new patent which would limit labor services to three days a week and lay the groundwork for eventually transforming these services into money payments. Kaunitz opposed the new patent, saying that it would be detrimental to the dignity of the queen and was not called for by the circumstances, but Joseph prevailed. On August 13, 1775, a new patent was issued in keeping with the ideas of Joseph.

Tactlessly, Joseph took the occasion to express opposition to Kaunitz's suggestion for raising money to compensate the nobility. When his mother tersely and angrily responded, Joseph declared his intention to resign. Understanding his mother's temperament as he did, Joseph probably used the threat of resignation to force her to his position and, in fact, Maria Theresa quickly surrendered. Kaunitz, having twice been rebuffed on the peasant problem, now declared his intention to withdraw from office. Maria Theresa prevailed upon him to stay, but to do so she had to express her willingness to prevent further incursions on the nobility's proprietary rights. Practically speaking, what this meant was the acceptance of the Robot Patent of 1775 as the basic and immutable definition of the manorial relationship. Kaunitz was too wise to believe that what had once been done could now be undone, but he was certain that further deterioration could be prevented at least as long as Maria Theresa lived. The patent of March 1, 1777, represented the protection Kaunitz sought, for while accepting the specific arrangements of the patent of 1775, it refuted the notion that further changes—for example, the translation of labor services into money rent—were imminent. In fact, the patent of 1775 had already proven to be inadequate primarily because it could not be enforced. The customary power of the lords on the estates could not be so easily undone despite the development of centralized power.

Kaunitz's position and Maria Theresa's acceptance of it could easily be interpreted as reactionary, as a desire to reestablish noble control of the peasantry. They did derive from a particular social conception which today may be labeled reactionary and often derided as "paternalism," or more appropriately in this instance "maternalism." It was maternalistic and Maria Theresa so conceived it, but it was a positive notion that had as one of its basic ingredients a deep and abiding concern for the welfare of the people who had been given into her care. Thus Maria Theresa was able to envisage reforms even more sweeping than Joseph intended, though she recognized the improbability of achieving them. This concern was clearly reflected in the other agricultural policies she advocated in the 1770's, measures aimed at improving the economic situation of the peasants.

Of special interest here is Maria Theresa's advocacy of the "Raab system," which William Wright has called "the most radical and promising agrarian reform of her reign."[17] The justification for this experiment was rooted in the populationist theory of Joseph von Sonnenfels, which led to the conclusion that in order to increase the agrarian population and make it fully productive, the serfs would have to be established on small independent holdings. While refusing to enforce so drastic a revision of the land-holding system on the reluctant nobility, Maria Theresa decided to experiment with the reform on her own lands, hoping that if it were successful the nobles would be encouraged to adopt it. The man responsible for conducting the experiment was Franz Anton von Raab, a member of the Commerce Commission who had submitted a detailed proposal on the subject. Maria Theresa gave Raab a free hand to carry out the reform on two Bohemian estates, Schurz and Schatzlar.

In brief, the Raab system abolished labor service (*robota*) and divided the estates into small hereditary leaseholds. In return, the peasant would pay a fee scaled to the amount of service he had owed and a rent fixed by a schedule based on four levels of land quality as identified by a careful land survey. Additionally, the peasants would purchase all the buildings and implements from the former estate over a ten-year period, again according to a set rate, and could buy the estate animals at auction.[18] In addition to determining payment, the quality of the land was also to determine the size of a leasehold; thus Raab recognized disparities produced by natural circumstances. For the crown the advantages were clear. The system eliminated the cost of operating the estate, thus making the revenue from fees and rents clear profit. The peasant, having a greater stake in the land, would work harder and productivity should therefore increase.

The increase in productivity would in turn strengthen the tax base.

Though Maria Theresa's own motives for favoring the Raab plan had much to do with her concern for the peasant, she was not displeased by the anticipation of economic benefit. Obviously she recognized the economic argument as her chief instrument in dealing with the nobility—and she hoped to convince all the nobility, even the Hungarians, to adopt the system for their own lands. From the beginning, despite minor difficulties, the reform appeared successful and Maria Theresa quickly empowered Raab to expand the system to other domainal estates in Bohemia (March, 1776) and by 1777 the system was the accepted pattern for the royal lands. Despite the apparent success, however, the nobility steadfastly refused to consider the Raab system as a viable alternative to the manorial system. Even some of the royal estate managers continued to oppose it. Believers in the idea of a fixed quantity of wealth, they were convinced that prosperity for the peasant could develop only at the expense of the noble. Contrarily, the nobles, also transcending the economic argument, regarded the reform as an attack on the status system which gave them prestige and power. Thus during Maria Theresa's reign the model which the Raab system provided was not widely emulated, though the cameral estates where it was sustained served as laboratories for the more sweeping changes Joseph attempted after 1780.

Economic policy in general increasingly demanded Maria Theresa's attention. On the one hand, the death of Francis had removed one of her most able advisers in this sphere; on the other, the impact of the Seven Years' War forced recognition of the flaws in the earlier interventionist policy. Only about one third of the war costs were covered by revenue and free subsidies, leaving the rest to be covered by credit. Not surprisingly, the state debt increased sharply (to 271 million gulden in 1763 and 376 million in 1780). To meet costs the government in 1762 and again in 1771 issued terminal paper notes as a stopgap, the first such issued in Central Europe and a policy in striking contrast to the usual procedure of debasing the silver, a measure which even the enlightened Frederick adopted.

More significant than this temporary measure was the general shift in policy which occurred as the result of agitation by Joseph and Kaunitz, among others, and was reflected in the economic theories of Joseph von Sonnenfels.[19] Sonnenfels regarded the people themselves as the most important economic resource and assumed that a population increase was the surest guarantee of an increase in political and economic power as well as of cultural development. While he maintained that the population level would never increase beyond the capabilities of the state to support it, he rejected the belief that the free play of economic forces would automatically benefit the state. Contrasted with genuine economic liberalism as it emerged in the writings of Adam Smith, Sonnenfels' neomercantilism seems quite restrictive, but in contrast to the stricter mercantilism of earlier years it seems quite free. It most certainly was in keeping with the theories of the Enlightenment, especially in its espousal of humanitarianism. Sonnenfels' ideas were not the official theories of the day but they were very influential in the formulation of economic policy because of their appeal to Joseph and even Kaunitz. Maria Theresa, by nature opposed to the secular utilitarianism underlying Sonnenfels' theories, nevertheless protected him from the rigors of censorship by declaring that he was to be permitted to write as his principles dictated. His ideas thus could be heard.

In practice the theory revealed its internal contradictions; it also encountered conflicts inherent in the Austrian system, notably a burgeoning tension between political and commercial interests and the peculiar dynamic existing among Maria Theresa, Joseph, and Kaunitz. In the latter regard, a significant and characteristic issue concerned tariffs. Kaunitz argued that prohibitive tariffs on foreign goods would promote smuggling rather than native industry. Joseph, on the other hand, maintained that Austria could not gain strength through an expansion of foreign trade, but must concentrate on building her own industry to supply her own needs. He urged the creation of some authority to supervise not only the commercial but the general economic policy of the state. In response, Maria Theresa in December, 1768, established a State Economic Council with Count Rudolf Chotek as the presiding officer, and with membership drawn from the various councils and committees involved in economic matters. This new council was to have supervision over all economic questions in the monarchy. Initially, the Council favored a "Buy Habsburg" policy which entailed creating tariff barriers against imports. By 1772, however, Maria Theresa had apparently decided that the prohibition of foreign goods had been carried too far. In spite of the personal pressure of the queen, it was not until May, 1773, that the Council took steps to ease the barriers, and even then the decision was not unanimous.

One aspect of Theresian economic policy that had particular political significance was its clear "anti-Hungarian" bias. The discouragement of industry in Hungary had initially been a pragmatic and temporary measure, but since the Hungarian Diet of 1764, when the Hungarian Estates and especially the magnates had resisted so firmly Maria Theresa's efforts to gain a larger appropriation, Maria Theresa had become less tolerant of Magyar privileges. She herself never singled Hungary out for retribution, but she was convinced that additional favors were not required. Kaunitz strongly seconded this conviction, for he clearly believed the government should impose economic restrictions on Hungary to put that troublesome land in its proper place politically.[20]

Maria Theresa had no desire to transform society. Rather, she wished to refine the social structure so that each group within it received justice and in turn acted justly. The educational reforms of 1765-1780 embodied this hierarchical principle. The actual proposals were the work of such men as Johann Anton von Pergen and Matthias Ignaz von Hess, and reflected the ideas of Kaunitz and even Joseph, but Maria Theresa undeniably approved the specific reforms. Pergen argued that the chief goal of education was to prepare people to serve the state as enlightened Christians, that the state should control all education and that the monastic orders should no longer be entrusted with teaching responsibilities. Apparently Pergen spoke for Kaunitz in enunciating these principles. Kaunitz himself insisted that the instruction of each class was to grow out of the particular purpose which that class served in society.[21] Education had three aspects—religious, moral, and vocational, of which the most fundamental was a morality conforming to each estate. Derived from philosophical principles of the Enlightenment, Kaunitz's views on education nonetheless converged with Maria Theresa's own, and in this instance, as in others, her more traditional but pragmatic conceptions blunted the philosophical predilections of her advisers.[22] Thus, for example, for Kaunitz (as for Joseph) religion served essentially a civic function and therefore he advocated secularizing all teaching. But in the General Law for the Schools of Austria (December 6, 1774), while state control was unmistakable, ecclesiastical authorities still conducted education: a typically Theresian touch.[23]

The General Law established a hierarchy of school types and prescribed a curriculum for each type consonant with the social need which it was to fulfill. While all schools were to offer instruction in religion and reading, the Trivial schools, in effect the local primary schools which would provide the sum and substance of education for the vast majority of the population, were to stress those things "written to form 'an honest citizen,' and to teach him thrift and management." Clearly operative here was the belief that too much education for the common people, or rather the wrong kind of education, was a dangerous thing. (Curiously, Joseph evinced this belief even more than Maria Theresa did.)

Generally, two other factors restricted the effectiveness of all educational reforms. The extension of state control did not create a state system of education. The local schools remained a parochial institution under the direction of the parish priest, though under fairly strict government supervision. Additionally, the reforms effected, on whatever level, applied only to the German-Bohemian lands and efforts to extend them throughout the monarchy failed. Consequently, the successes of Maria Theresa's educational policy were isolated: the elementary schools, the medical schools, and the training of young noblemen for bureaucratic service represent its best fruits. The limitations were many, with higher education suffering the most. The lack of a comprehensive reform in higher education in turn meant that the resources to staff the remainder of the program were not entirely adequate.

Undergirding the hierarchical structure which Maria Theresa envisioned, if she did not establish it, was a principle of equality: not that all men had equal rights, but that the rights of each individual were equally sacred and that the monarch's obligation to protect and preserve those rights was equal for all. Maria Theresa's conception of her role as the mother of her people embodied this principle most richly. Within the family, each child had a task to fill, determined in part by order of birth and sex; Maria Theresa sought to provide for each as the potential demanded, but she wished to love them all equally and to strive equally for the welfare of each. Translated to her dominions, this maternalism implied an abiding concern for the welfare of her people, a concern arising not from an abstract or philosophical humanitarianism but from the intensely personal spirit of motherhood. Joseph's aspiration to be a servant of his people differed not only in gender but in intrinsic spirit.

The English observer Wraxall commented in 1777 that "Maria Theresa, sinking in years; divided between her religious observances, and her civil duties; occupied alternately in business of state, and in exercises of devotion; hopes to pass the evening of her stormy reign in peace, surrounded by her numerous family."[24] But the family was scattered, the circle restricted now to woeful women and a joyless widower. The court was not a cheerful place. Maria Theresa's private life reduced itself to paper, page upon page of letters to her children, and the leaves of innumerable baroque devotionals. Having devoted herself in her vigor to public life, she now in her frailty had only that, and its parameters were set by the intricate web of her relations with Joseph and Kaunitz. Vacillation frequently marked her deliberations and periods of passivity tempered her authority. But she struggled to do her duty, borne on by the elusive hope "to pass the evening of her stormy reign in peace."

CHAPTER IX

The Co-regency with Joseph:
Foreign Affairs

THE TREATY OF HUBERTUSBURG, WHICH HAD BROUGHT THE SEVEN Years' War to an unsatisfactory end, did not dissolve the Habsburg-Bourbon alliance. Though the immediate goal of the alliance, the reacquisition of Silesia, had eluded Austria, the basic premises upon which the relationship had been founded, that Prussia was the Habsburgs' archenemy and that the maritime powers could not provide satisfactory support against this foe, remained unaltered. Without hesitation, Maria Theresa accepted the maintenance of the French alliance, for she had no doubt that Frederick was the chief threat to her safety. The politics of the marital arrangements she made for her children provide the most vivid proof of her commitment to the alliance. No less than five of the betrothals were intended to reinforce the Habsburg-Bourbon relationship. Not surprisingly in 1764 Kaunitz firmly reiterated the government's view that the French alliance was an integral part of the Austrian state system.[1] There was, however, less agreement concerning the future uses of the alliance.

On this question Maria Theresa disagreed fundamentally with Joseph and Kaunitz, a disagreement which G.P. Gooch has characterized as a "conflict between the instinct of adventure and the slogan of safety first."[2] For Maria Theresa the years of turmoil had dulled the desire for revenge against Frederick and slackened the ambition to reassert her historic rights to Silesia. She was no longer willing to risk the dangers of war. Joseph and Kaunitz, on the other hand, were willing to take the risk. To them the real intention of the Bourbon alliance, to protect and strengthen Austria's great-power status, required the use of all the instruments of international politics, including war or at least the threat of war. Had Joseph and Kaunitz agreed entirely, they might have overcome Maria Theresa's resistance to an active, aggressive foreign policy. Had they agreed, the easy description of the co-regency as a "division of labor" in which Maria Theresa tended the garden at home while Joseph conducted relations with the neighbors might well be more accurate than it actually is. But there were profound differences between Joseph and Kaunitz and in that fact rests much of the explanation for Maria Theresa's ultimate authority in things foreign as well as domestic. That authority was not unshaken and it was less firm, but it persisted. A study of the crucial problems of foreign policy at the time—the Polish partition of 1772 and the Bavarian succession—reveals its nature and extent.

Polish power had ceased to be a critical factor in European politics in the seventeenth century, but Poland continued to occupy a significant place in the plans of other European rulers. Indeed, the election of Frederick Augustus, Elector of Saxony, as King of Poland in 1697 and Russia's emergence on the European scene increased Poland's importance. In 1733 the great Continental powers had warred over the monarchial succession in Poland. In 1763, with the Seven Years' War barely ended, the death of Augustus III (1733-1763) left the Polish throne vacant again.[3] Maria Theresa's policy was quite simple: though preferring that the Saxons continue to hold the Polish crown and that the country remain intact, Austria could not afford a war and she would avoid any issue which might cause one. Thus with Russian troops on hand to guide the Polish Diet in its selection, Maria Theresa recognized that only counterforce could prevent the election of Stanislas Poniatowski, Catherine's former lover. Unwilling to invoke force, Maria Theresa contented herself with the fact that Polish unity was not violated as the Diet elected Poniatowski (September 7, 1764). Maria Theresa's goals at this point were clearly more limited than those of her chancellor, Kaunitz. She desired peace; he desired to maintain Austria's influence in Central European affairs. Kaunitz quickly concluded that Poniatowski wished to be more independent than either Catherine or Frederick had intended, but in order to assert such independence he required Austrian support. To Kaunitz this was an opportunity to separate Poland from Russia, but Maria Theresa, while willing and even eager to recognize the Polish king, hesitated to display too much friendliness. A crisis developed when the king tried to use the con-

tinuation of the General Confederation to enact extensive
reforms, including the abandonment of the *liberum veto* and
the assertion of religious unity, two subjects on which Catherine
and Frederick had strong opinions. Confronted by their harsh
reaction to Poniatowski's program, Maria Theresa issued pious
statements about protecting friendly nations from the violent
whims of foreign monarchs, but offered no aid. As a result, the
Polish Diet heeded the dictates of Russia. Austria's policy was
universally dismissed as the consequence of weakness, a weakness
reiterated in 1767 when Maria Theresa refused to intervene as
Catherine ordered troops into Poland to enforce her policy and
thereby ignited a religious civil war.

Throughout this period, Austrian policy rested on the continuation of the alliance with France, the prevention of a partition, and the avoidance of war. Kaunitz, conscious of Russian
power, believed that Austria could most easily preserve Poland
by acting as a co-guarantor of the Polish constitution with Russia.
The alliance with France, however, obstructed this policy.
Choiseul had concluded that France should limit Russian power,
and he found a ready listener to his proposals in Turkey. The
growing entente between Versailles and the Porte confronted
Austria with the prospect of being dragged into a war with
Russia to preserve her friendship with France. To preserve that
friendship without war, Kaunitz determined to separate Prussia
from Russia, convinced that Catherine would not go to war
without Frederick's aid, and that France would regard the
dissolution of the Russo-Prussian relationship as a sufficient
check on Catherine's power.

Since the Treaty of Hubertusburg, Austro-Prussian relations
had been remarkably amicable. Without surrendering her personal
dislike and distrust of Frederick, Maria Theresa conscientiously
avoided antagonizing him because of her intense desire for
peace. To promote an even closer accord with Frederick,
Kaunitz tried to arrange a personal meeting between Frederick
and Joseph. Expressing displeasure about such an encounter,
Maria Theresa refused to approve the proposal. The plan failed,
however, only when Joseph finally rejected it, apparently because
he did not wish to be Kaunitz's errand boy. Maria Theresa explained the failure by saying, "The interview ... did not take
place, since providence did not wish it ... The proverb is
verified: man proposes, God disposes."[4] A subsequent effort

to arrange a meeting also failed, this time Joseph making very explicit his dissatisfaction with Kaunitz's overprotective attitude.

In October, 1768, a Russo-Turkish war broke out, the French ambassador having goaded on the war hawks at the Turkish court. Maria Theresa reiterated her desire for peace, and argued that Austria had nothing to gain from the war, indeed that the very fact the war was being fought was to her disadvantage. As the crisis continued, Maria Theresa advocated a policy of strict neutrality, though hinting that further intervention into Poland might induce her to reconsider that policy. Kaunitz had no wish to go to war, but wanted to avoid a public renunciation of force which would limit the flexibility of Austrian diplomacy. Nor did he accept the idea of strict noninvolvement, rather insisting that Austria must play a crucial role in any negotiations concerning Central Europe. Kaunitz proposed an agreement uniting the interests of Austria, Turkey, and Prussia. Joseph dismissed the project as impractical because the benefits promised Turkey and Prussia were inadequate to induce them to make a commitment to Austria. When Maria Theresa concurred, the project was abandoned. Rebuffed, Kaunitz quickly returned to the idea of a meeting between Frederick and Joseph. Maria Theresa, eager to prevent the war from spreading, approved and Joseph followed suit. Clearly at this point the chancellor had assumed the initiative for Austrian policy; the monarchs merely acted as restraints on his enthusiasm.

By the time the first meeting of the kings was held, August, 1769, in Neisse, the Polish situation had deteriorated rapidly. In response to sporadic forays by Polish forces into Austrian and Prussian lands (1769), the Vienna court on Kaunitz's recommendation had established a military cordon around Spisz (Zips), a congeries of thirteen towns near the Hungarian-Polish border which had been under Polish control since 1412. Frederick accepted Austria's assertion that this was a temporary step, and indeed he followed Austria's example by establishing a similar cordon near Elblag and Warmier. In the summer of 1770, Austria expanded her military occupation and then in December, 1770, formally proclaimed the incorporation of Spisz into the kingdom of Hungary. On numerous occasions thereafter, Kaunitz asserted his opposition to both these maneuvers, insisting that Austria must avoid any action which might provoke a partition. The crucial decision to incorporate Spisz was loosely ascribed to the "Austrian court." Probably the decisions were products of machinations by a military clique, especially Marshal Lacy, in response to Russian successes in Poland.[5] Following the signing of the partition agreement in 1772, Maria Theresa wote to Lacy:

> The St. Petersburg couriers have brought back the unhappy partitions, signed. It is to you that I owe this great advantage, if such it be. What is certain is that you formed the plan and were able to demand so much and thus to procure this gain for the state, without being implicated in the question whether it is just or not.[6]

Joseph was apparently the target of the military clique's influence. At least his attitude during the crisis appeared similar to theirs, and he pressed both Maria Theresa and Kaunitz to act more aggressively.[7] He may have been responsible for the extension of the cordon (the military was after all his special province) but at no time during the crisis did he appear to have full control of Austrian policy. Kaunitz, who seemingly held the initiative in formulating Austrian policy, clearly opposed the partitions and moved to secure a share for Austria only when it became inevitable.[8] Maria Theresa was adamant in her desire to avoid war and she opposed a partition, yet apparently she issued the order to "reincorporate" Spisz. In her own mind she distinguished between Spisz and other areas subsequently included in the Austrian sphere (the Habsburgs had a formal, albeit feeble, claim to Spisz). This distinction hardly exonerates her, but to dismiss her actions as mere hypocrisy is to oversimplify. Her persistent opposition to a partition of Poland led to an alliance with Turkey (July, 1771) aimed at forcing Russia to a quick peace. As late as November, 1771, she reasserted her opposition to the dismemberment of Poland, but by then neither Catherine nor Frederick could be deterred from their course. Given the fact of the partition, Maria Theresa still preferred that Austria not profit from Poland's misery: if she must take lands, let Prussia have her share in Poland and return to her the lost province of Silesia. When Frederick refused to consider the possibility, Maria Theresa resigned herself to acquiring whatever the craft of Kaunitz made possible.

In mid-February, 1772, Maria Theresa instructed her chancellor:

All partitions are unjust, and at bottom harmful to us. . . . Never
in my life have I found myself in such anxiety. When all my lands
had been attacked, I steeled myself to resistance because I could
trust in my right and in the aid of God. But in the present case,
where there is not only no right on my side, but alliances, justice
and fairness are against me, I have no peace left, but only anxiety
and reproach. . . . Trust and faith, the greatest jewels and truest
strength of a monarch, are lost forever. . . . I cannot abstain from
repeating again: I am not strong enough to rule by myself. Therefore, and not without deepest sorrow, I allow you to pursue your
own path.[9]

As if in response to Kaunitz's subsequent argument that it would
be as foolish for Austria to stand by without participating as
to try to prevent the partition by force, she noted in a memo
entitled "Jeremiads":

A Prince has no rights other than those possessed by any private
individual; the greatness and maintenance of his State will not enter
into the balance on the day when we shall all have to appear to give
our accounts. . . . Let us be regarded as fools rather than knaves.[10]

But Kaunitz, though he had opposed the partition, was a spec-
ulative opportunist and he took full advantage of the situation,
thus acquiring far more for Austria than originally anticipated.
Either Catherine or the French ambassador sourly remarked of
Maria Theresa, "The more she weeps, the more she takes."

For Austria, the ultimate result of the partition was a deepen-
ing involvement with non-German lands that would have important consequences for her subsequent development. Of
more immediate concern was the problem of authority in the
co-regency; the monarchy was experiencing a crisis and
Austrian policy was adrift. At no time during the long struggle
over the partition did Maria Theresa control Habsburg policy
as firmly as she had done before. Though she retained the final
decision-making power, her expressed fear that she was losing
control had substance. Contrarily, Joseph, displaying a more
aggressive attitude than his mother and assuming a greater role
in the making of foreign policy, failed to determine the course of
events. At this critical juncture in Central European affairs, the
Habsburg monarchy lacked decisive leadership, and only the
craft of Kaunitz had made the undesired settlement a beneficent
one for Austria. Thus in external affairs at least a "crazy

multiplicity of authority" marked the government. The subsequent problem of the Bavarian succession verifies this, for while
it illustrates Joseph's assumption of initiative, it also demonstrates
the persistence of Maria Theresa's authority in foreign affairs.[11]

The proposal to extend Habsburg control over Bavaria was
not novel. In Maria Theresa's own reign a proposal had been
made as early as 1742 to exchange Habsburg lands in the Netherlands or Italy for Bavaria. Even in the midst of the Polish
turmoil Kaunitz was busily preparing for the Bavarian succession
crisis. (The elector of Bavaria, Maximilian Joseph, was childless
and his brother Clemens died in 1770.) When Maximilian
Joseph died in late 1777, however, it was Joseph who took the
lead. The European powers were then distracted by the American Revolution and the closest legal heir to Bavaria, Karl Theodor of the Palatinate, had little interest in Bavaria. Negotiations between him and Austria, begun in November, 1776,
produced a convention (January 2, 1778) recognizing Austrian
claims.

Kaunitz advised Maria Theresa about the negotiations, but
she was not directly involved. Periodically, in notes to the
chancellor or to her son, she expressed concern about, but not
open opposition to, the discussions. On hearing of the Elector's
death, however, she vigorously emphasized her opposition to
any steps which would open Austria to attack, her disavowal of
any policy aimed at acquiring lands to which she did not have
rightful title, and her determination that war was an instrument
of policy she would not condone. Yet she recognized that she
herself was not in full control of policy. In a conversation with the
French ambassador, Breteuil, she openly expressed her fear
that Austria might again be plunged into war shattering her
hopes to end her days in peace. When Breteuil asked whether
Austria would send troops into Bavaria, "She responded 'I do not
know,' with the tone, the gesture and the look of a person who
wished me to understand that it did not depend on her alone."[12]
The prospect of war was not much more disquieting than the
near certainty that in a war France would remain neutral. Despite
all the labors of her reign, it appeared that she would close her
career as friendless and isolated as she had begun it.

The crisis deepened when Karl of Zweibrücken, the heir of
Karl Theodor, sought Prussian aid to prevent the alienation of
his claims. Karl Theodor in turn raised his demands for com-

pensation. Enlivened by the mounting danger, Maria Theresa tried to reassert her authority. On March 14, 1778, she wrote at length to Joseph:

The disadvantages and dangers which I foresaw from the moment we marched into Bavaria are all too clearly becoming realities, and are growing to such an extent that I would be unworthy to bear the title of a Queen and of a mother if I did not take the measures which circumstances require without consideration of the consequences for myself.
The question is nothing short of the ruin of our dynasty and the monarchy, even of a complete revolution in Europe. No measure is too strong to end this misfortune in time. I will commit myself willingly to anything, even to the dishonoring of my name. One can reproach me for being foolish, weak and cowardly; nothing will deter me from preserving Europe from this threatening dilemma; there is no better way for me to expend the rest of my unhappy days.

Proceeding, she analyzed pessimistically the military capabilities of the monarchy and the magnitude of the task which a commitment to war would create, and then concluded by asserting:

After everything which I have just said, I must declare to you that I cannot continue to act against my conscience and against my conviction; this is not the result of ill will, nor personal cowardice. I feel as strong as I did thirty years ago, but never will I cooperate in the ruin of my dynasty and my state.

Added to this letter, written in the hand of her secretary Pichler, is a note in Maria Theresa's own hand which says:

If the war breaks out, depend on me no longer. I will withdraw to the Tyrol and there end my days, and occupy myself with nothing but weeping and lamenting for the sad fortune of my dynasty and my people and conclude my unhappy life in a Christian manner.[13]

During the summer of 1778 she continued to bombard Joseph with pleas to seek a reconciliation, but the armies took the field. Rather than withdrawing, however, Maria Theresa sent a diplomatic mission to Prussian headquarters to negotiate a peace. Frederick sought to take advantage of the disunity at the Austrian court, until Catherine intervened as mediator and gained approval for a peace congress to meet at Teschen.
The desultory "Potato War" and the endless diplomatic skir-

mishings that accompanied it ended with Austria acquiring the *Innviertel*, but having to renounce her claims to Bavaria. For Joseph and Kaunitz the Treaty of Teschen represented a defeat, for they had to abandon their original plan of expansion and to see their hopes for an extension of Austria's German power base frustrated. The crisis also demonstrated the weakness of the French alliance and thus raised the question of a reorientation of Austria's alliance system. To Maria Theresa, however, the signing of the treaty was a glorious event. To celebrate the peace, on May 23, 1779, Pentecost, she listened to a *Te Deum* in St. Stephen's. Afterwards she wrote to Kaunitz: "I have today gloriously ended my career with a *Te Deum;* whatever the cost, I am overcome by joy because with His help peace has been restored to my lands. There is nothing left for me to desire."[14]

The war, or more accurately, the peace negotiations, had a more profound impact on Europe in general than on Germany in particular. Catherine achieved what she had intended: her mediation of the conflict had projected Russia into a position of leadership in the affairs of Europe. The combination of the increase of Russian prestige and the indecisiveness of France prompted Joseph to think carefully about improving relations with the Russian empire. For that reason, Joseph in 1780 proposed a trip to Russia to meet Catherine. More than any other aspect of foreign policy, even the Bavarian project, the attempted rapprochement with Russia marked the beginning of Joseph's independent reign. To be sure, many of the values which Joseph recognized in such an understanding were shared by Kaunitz, and it was the chancellor who overcame Maria Theresa's opposition to the proposed interview. Begrudgingly she consented, but then turned her own attention to a matter closer to her own heart, the election of her youngest son, Maximilian, as coadjutor to the Archbishop of Cologne.[15]

Until 1761 the Archbishopric—and therefore the Electorship —of Cologne had been a Wittelsbach monopoly. After the death of the Elector Klemens August, however, Maximilian Friedrich von Königsegg-Rothenfels had assumed the title. A relatively weak figure, Maximilian Friedrich was chosen as a compromise candidate. As he grew older the question arose whether he should have a coadjutor to guarantee the succession and so avoid a crisis on his death. The logical Habsburg candidate was Maximilian

Franz. Already Grand Master of the Teutonic Order, he was pledged to a celibate life, thus the change to clerical status appeared to be no great sacrifice. Maria Theresa, however, at first resisted the suggestion. On the one hand she felt this course would fix too firmly his future—he could withdraw from the Order if he desired and lead a normal secular life—and on the other hand she was not certain he possessed the dignity of person necessary to fill so high a station in the Church. Here again we find reflected both Maria Theresa's concern for the happiness of her children and her realistic appraisal of their character and ability.

In 1778, however, while serving in the abortive Potato War, Maximilian fell ill and it was soon obvious that the continuation of his military career was not possible. In 1779 the question of the coadjutorship of Cologne was reopened and Maria Theresa now gave her consent. Indeed through her correspondence with Marie Antoinette she managed to influence the French government to approve the election and so deprive Frederick of his chief support in resisting the Habsburg effort. Characteristically, however, Maria Theresa obtained from the Papacy a dispensation which permitted Max Franz to delay taking his final vows for five years.

Despite her preoccupation with this dynastic matter, Maria Theresa did not lose sight of larger issues of foreign policy and thus exercised a decisive role in Austrian policy in regard to the American Revolution.[16] In 1778 William Lee, one of a number of men dispatched by the Continental Congress to seek the recognition of European courts, arrived in Vienna. Eager and naïve, Lee blundered about the Habsburg capital with little success, despite the friendly aid of the French Ambassador, Baron de Breteuil. Even if Lee had been a skilled diplomat, however, prospects of success would have been slight. With the Bavarian crisis at hand, Austria had no desire to involve herself in a problem regarded as strictly the affair of England and France. The sanction of the French was in fact a detriment: Kaunitz interpreted the intercessions of Breteuil as an attempt to embroil Austria with England, and so refused to receive Lee officially, snubbing him when social encounters were unavoidable. Heartily endorsing the behavior of Kaunitz, Maria Theresa herself refused an audience to Lee and followed this by banning all trade between the Austrian Netherlands and the "rebel colonies." Joseph vigorously seconded his mother. Maria Theresa was less concerned about the effect Austrian policy would have on relations with England than she was affronted by the nature of the American cause. Though expressing her warm regard for George III and his government, she observed to Joseph that while France would be antagonized by Austrian policy, England would not attach great importance to it. Her action was not taken to placate England so much as it was to register her profound disapproval of an illegitimate government.

Yet within a year Austria offered her services as a mediator in the conflict. On May 15, 1779, only two days after the conclusion of the Treaty of Teschen, Maria Theresa wrote to her son-in-law Louis XVI, proposing Austrian mediation, supposedly as a return for France's contributions at Teschen. Four days later, Kaunitz made the same proposal to the British. (The desire "to return the favor" was probably not entirely friendly.) The Austrian offer did not come at a propitious moment. In April, Spain had agreed to come into the war. Heartened by this prospect and fearful lest Austria might use her role as mediator to effect a rapprochement with England, France politely declined Austria's good offices. The rejection stimulated a new wave of anti-French feeling at the Vienna court, but neither Maria Theresa nor Kaunitz quickly abandoned their efforts. The queen besieged her daughter with concerned letters and Kaunitz constantly prodded the Austrian ambassador in Paris, Count Mercy d'Argentau. Both England and France continued to rebuff the Austrian overtures. Not until 1781 would Austria become prominent in the diplomacy of the American Revolution. By then Joseph II ruled alone.

By the late 1770's Joseph had begun to consolidate his position in the government and thus to resolve the crisis of authority so apparent in the Polish question. Maria Theresa, however, retained the power to determine policy, as evidenced by her intervention into the Bavarian adventure, and the diplomacy of the American Revolution demonstrated her continued ability to determine priorities. But the flame was burning out.

Conclusion

On July 4, 1780, Prince Charles of Lorraine, Maria Theresa's brother-in-law and her regent in the Netherlands, died. The loss was a grievous one for the queen and made her acutely conscious of the imminence of her own death. She was then sixty-three years old, hardly young, but not ancient by any measure. Her great rival, Frederick, was five years older and would live another half-dozen years. Maria Theresa, however, felt old. With so many of those closest to her long dead, the loneliness of the twilight years enveloped her. Only Kaunitz remained. Though he retained the energy of the young and would live to serve as chief minister for both Joseph II and Leopold II, his personal eccentricities increasingly resembled those of an old maid; and he never lost that ultimate reserve which prevented him from providing his sovereign with any real companionship. The somberness of the family court, in mourning then for fifteen years, the sounds of childhood and youth replaced by the querulous mutterings of her maiden daughters, made more meaningful the conviction of her faith that this world was but the foyer to the next and encouraged the funereal aspects of her piety.

In her letters she referred increasingly to her ill health and loneliness. In October she prepared her will. Yet she contemplated the prospect of death without terror. Her one fear was that she might slip into unconsciousness and so be unable to make her last confession. But, just as she had met the awesome obligations which had come to her as ruler of the Habsburg dominions, so she met this final obligation of her faith. On November 19 she was forced to bed with a heavy cold and her condition steadily worsened. Despite persistent discomfort she made no complaint, appearing to be more concerned with the effect of her illness on those around her than with her own suffering. On November 28 she received the Last Sacrament and then called her family to her bedside. Five of her ten surviving children—Joseph, Maximilian, Maria Anna, Maria Christina, and Maria Elizabeth—and her favorite son-in-law, Christina's husband, Albert of Saxe-Teschen, were there to receive her last blessing. Told that she should rest, she replied: "I will not sleep, I wish to see death come."[1] She wrote a letter to Kaunitz thanking him for his long and loyal service—characteristically even at this point he would not surrender his aversion to entering a sickroom. Toward nine on the evening of November 29, with Joseph at her side, she died.

At her death there was a sense of relief among many Austrians. The long reign had obscured the image of the beautiful young queen leading Austria through its darkest hour, of the loving wife and mother, who because of the grace of God and the obligations of her dynasty took up the burdens of state. More vivid was the figure of the tired and aging monarch, reluctant to rule and yet reluctant to cede authority to her heir. Now the problem of authority was solved: Joseph was free to embark on his program in earnest. The frenetic quality of the next decade was to induce many to look back on the Theresian period more fondly, but a final evaluation of Maria Theresa's reign does not depend on any comparison with the reign of her son. To esteem Theresian Austria one need not regard it wistfully as that happier time before Joseph. In its own right it was the most important reign in Habsburg history.

Invariably biographers conclude that in spirit Maria Theresa continued the "Age of the Baroque" and thus seemed a misfit in the world of the Enlightenment, the age of such rulers as Frederick II, Catherine II, and her own son. To be sure, she emerged from the soil of "baroque"—Austria, South Germany, and Catholicism—yet she was part of the epoch in which she lived, not of a past age. She breathed the air of the eighteenth century though she did not succumb to it. The Theresian enlightenment differed from the Frederician or Josephian enlightenment just as the personalities of the three monarchs differed. Her enlightenment was contained within the limits of her piety; she was bound by the persisting spirit of the Counter-Reformation. Ambitious and possessed of the strongest self-conviction, she yet was not consumed by the spirit of adventure and power as was Catherine. No monarch of her age had such royal bearing or such devotion to her people.

In her reform program, Maria Theresa remained distinctly

pragmatic. Her pragmatism encompassed not only the ability to comprehend the specific needs of her monarchy, but also a striking talent for assessing what was feasible. To her, politics was certainly the art of the possible and one historian has characterized her as "primarily a politician concerned with the impact of her reforms on politically influential persons and groups, and not—or not simply—an administrator striving for consistency and precision in the formulation and application of general rules."[2] Similarly, in foreign affairs, she was not completely doctrinaire, but was willing to compromise even with the hated Frederick.[3] Inclined to proceed by consultation and compromise, she was not wont to dream the impossible dream. Unlike Joseph, she was not propelled by the impulse to carry to its ultimate conclusion the abstract logic implied by her reforms. Maria Theresa tried to do that which the good of the monarchy required and she sensed that that which was most rational was not always most reasonable.

She also recognized that the good of the monarchy and the welfare of the dynasty were not synonymous. For her the old dynasticism was no longer viable. Again, however, her maternalistic and therefore intensely personal view led her to conceive the monarchy as an extended family rather than as a rationalized power state. Again and again in her letters Maria Theresa gave expression to her conviction that trust was the essential bond of a family, whether it be the narrow family of blood or the broader familial gathering of ruler and people. On her deathbed she instructed Joseph: "... My children alone still are, and will always be mine; I deliver them to you, be to them a father. I shall die contented if you promise to take that office upon you."[4] She spoke of her kin; she could have been speaking of her people. Thus in the contest between Joseph's will to rule and her devotion to the good of her people, she always finally refused to abdicate. Thus also, while her father, bound to the old dynastic view, could not reform, and her son, driven by a vision of an enlightened future, could not conserve, Maria Theresa lovingly and devoutly did both. "For Maria Theresa was a great reformer, even a revolutionary if one wishes, but a revolutionary with a sense of heart and a prevailing kindness and a very clear awareness of the limits of the possible as well as of the human and technical qualities of her co-workers."[5]

At the close of her reign Austria had still to be reckoned as one of the great powers.[6] In part, the measure of this accomplishment is relative. Austria's power had declined in absolute terms, but so had that of France and Turkey, two of her traditional rivals. Furthermore, despite its failings, the Franco-Austrian alliance of 1756 survived and in the east Austria had become a supporter of Turkey's territorial integrity. The rise of England to preeminence was tempered in Continental affairs by her insularity, while the increasing power of Russia and Prussia, on the one hand a clear threat to Austria, had the paradoxical effect of producing a geographic drift of European diplomacy toward the east and so encouraging Austria's claim to great-power status. Maria Theresa had not voided Frederick's claims to such status, but she had preserved the Habsburg empire from disintegration. She had not blunted Catherine's drive for power, but she had obtained a buffer against Russia's westward expansion toward the Carpathians.

Within Germany, Prussia's emergence weakened Austria, and the polarization of power between Austria and Prussia, Habsburg and Hohenzollern, was a factor of crucial importance for the future. Maria Theresa's very success in consolidating monarchial control within her dominions, when coupled with the loss of Silesia and the failure to acquire compensatory lands in Germany, biased the polarization and thus heavily influenced the solution of the German unification question in the nineteenth century. Friedrich Heer has commented:

The loss of the rich Silesian territories jolted the old Holy Roman Empire out of the ellipse it had formerly described between the male-female, Catholic-Protestant, poles. The Old Empire had been "unattached," "broad," flexible, organic, multicolored; these qualities perished in the fall.[7]

Within the Habsburg lands, the Theresian reforms consolidated the state, but they also delineated its most pressing problem of the future: the special status of Hungary. The differing modes of acceptance of the Pragmatic Sanction in Hungary and in the non-Hungarian lands had already given a legal quality to the Austro-Hungarian dualism; the reforms gave it a political reality because they were largely restricted to the non-Hungarian lands. Maria Theresa's expression of trust in the Magyar nobility at the beginning of her reign and her continued cultivation of them effectively denationalized the Hungarian magnates, but the large mass of the nobility were untouched by her appeals. They remained quiescent, however, because their privileges were not infringed on by the queen's reforms. Joseph's failure to create a unitary state was to confirm the dualism.

One is easily drawn to viewing her as a transitional monarch whose reign served as the bridge over the troubled waters marking the shift from the dynastic to the modern state. Within that interpretive scheme, Maria Theresa's success as a reformer derives from the fact that, sharing the assumptions of the past but impelled by practical reality, she could make great changes with minimal threat to stability. Ultimately, however, she undermined the foundations of the society she sought to preserve. This assessment implies a negative judgment on her reign: that, limited by the encumbrances of the past, Maria Theresa was unable to progress further than she did; and that, ultimately a conservative, she could not finally envision the liberal modern state. But perhaps she envisioned it all too well and found it wanting.[8] In our age, when the centralized bureaucratic state and the rationale of power have lost some of their nineteenth-century appeal, her hesitations and doubts seem more attractive. Was she in reality merely defending an old order based on rank and privilege? Or was she defending a conception of society rooted in an appreciation for the spiritual qualities of man and the requirements of justice? Maria Theresa would hardly understand liberal notions of equality and freedom, but she was far from being a mere law-and-order candidate. Viewed in this perspective, her reign appears not a way station on the road to the modern state, but an alternative, one no more durable perhaps, but also perhaps no less satisfactory.

As for Maria Theresa herself, Friedrich Walter has averred: "She succeeded in doing what no other great woman in history accomplished: she became an indisputable ruler without ever denying her femininity and she was always a woman without forgetting her imperial dignity. She attained the great goal which she had set for herself—as empress-queen she was always the universal and first mother of her dominions."[9] As this brief study has attempted to show, Maria Theresa embodied the monarchy. However much she owed the men she gathered around her, Maria Theresa gave purpose and direction to the state. Even in declining years as her impatient heir sought a greater role,

Maria Theresa, moved by native shrewdness, a profound sense of vocation, and maternal instincts, remained the final authority. It was she who ruled, and her biography is an integral part of Austria's history.

Notes and References

CHAPTER I

1. For a discussion of the reign of Charles VI and the Sanction, see Oswald Redlich, *Das Werden einer Grossmacht: Österreich 1700-1740* (Vienna, 1942); for the Sanction, see Gustav Turba, *Die pragmatische Sanktion, mit besonderer Rücksicht auf die Ländern der Stephanskrone* (Vienna, 1906), and *Die Grundlagen der Pragmatischen Sanktion* (Vienna, 1911-12); for an English translation of the Sanction and related documents, see C. A. Macartney, ed., *The Habsburg and Hohenzollern Dynasties in the Seventeenth and Eighteenth Centuries* (New York, 1970), pp. 82-94.

2. Frederick II of Prussia, *Histoire de mon Temps* (London, 1789), pt. 2, p. 51.

3. *Geschichte Maria Theresias* (Vienna, 1863), I, 13. [Hereafter Arneth]. This is still the best work available on the reign.

4. E.g. Peter Reinhold, *Maria Theresia* (Wiesbaden, 1957), p. 20. See also Robert Pick, *Empress Maria Theresa: The Earlier Years, 1717-1757* (New York, 1966), ch. II; and most recently, Edward Crankshaw, *Maria Theresa* (London, 1969). For a brief introduction to the reign, see C. A. Macartney, *Maria Theresa and the House of Austria* (London, 1969). The best German-language biography is Eugen Guglia, *Maria Theresia: Ihr Leben und ihre Regierung* (Munich, 1917), 2 vols. Another of note is Heinrich Kretschmayr, *Maria Theresia* (Gotha, 1925). There have been several French biographies of Maria Theresa, but none of any particular merit.

5. *Bilder aus Vergangenheit* (Frankfurt -a. -M., 1956), pp. 11-14.

6. For detailed discussions of the baroque concept in relation to Austrian history, see Robert Kann, *A Study in Austrian Intellectual History* (New York, 1960), pp. 1-49; and Therese Schüssel, *Kultur des Barock in Österreich* (Graz, 1960). For a critique of the concept, see Louis Menashe, "Historians Define the Baroque: Notes on a Problem of Art and Social History," *Comparative Studies in Society and History*, VII, 333-42.

7. See Anna Coreth, *Pietas Austriaca. Ursprung und Entwicklung barocker Frommigkeit in Österreich* (Vienna, 1959).

8. Helmut Tschol, "Gottfried Philipp Spanagel und die Geschichtsunterricht Maria Theresias," *Zeitschrift für Katholische Theologie* (1961), LXXXIII, 214.

9. Tschol, p. 221. Spanagel's preference for the imperial over the papal power was not arbitrary nor merely antiquarian, but was rooted very directly in the conflict between Vienna and Rome in Italy during the War of the Spanish Succession. Cf. Adam Wandruszka, *Österreich und Italien im 18. Jahrhundert* (Vienna, 1963), ch. 2.

10. Arneth, I, 7.

11. There is available a biography of Francis which provides an interesting characterization, but otherwise is of limited value. F. Hennings, *Und Sitzet zur linken Hand* (Vienna, 1961).

12. Josef Kallbrunner, ed., *Kaiserin Maria Theresias Politisches Testament* (Munich, 1952), p. 47.

13. J. Alexander Mahan, *Maria Theresa of Austria* (New York, 1932), pp. 35-36.

14. For an excellent biography of Prince Eugene in English, see Nicholas Henderson, *Prince Eugene of Savoy* (London, 1964). The most comprehensive study is Max Braubach, *Eugen von Savoyen. Eine Biographie* (Vienna, 1963-65), 5 vols.

15. Arneth, I, 53. For a detailed study of the diplomacy leading up to this unhappy peace, see Lavender Cassels, *The Struggle for the Ottoman Empire* (London, 1966).

CHAPTER II

1. William Coxe, *History of the House of Austria* (London, 1882), III, 189.

2. Arneth, I, 25.

3. Thomas Carlyle, *History of Friedrich the Second called Frederick the Great* (New York, n.d.), IV, 175.

4. *Politisches Testament*, also Friedrich Walter, ed., *Maria Theresia. Briefe und Aktenstücke in Auswahl* (Darmstadt, 1968), pp. 63-97 and 108-30. Arneth originally discovered and published these documents, *Archiv für österreichische Geschichte* [hereafter AÖG], XLVII (1871), 284 ff. The documents are undated but internal evidence indicates that Maria Theresa prepared the first one in 1749-1750 and the second in 1755-1756. For an English translation of the earlier document, see Macartney, *The Habsburg and Hohenzollern Dynasties*, pp. 94-132. For the reader's convenience, subsequent references to this document will be to this translation where applicable.

5. For a study of French policy at this time, see Arthur M. Wilson, *French Policy during the Administration of Cardinal Fleury* (Cambridge, 1936).

6. On Frederick, see Gerhard Ritter, *Frederick the Great. A Historical Profile* (Berkeley, 1968). Translated from the third German edition (Heidelberg, 1954). Jochen Klepper presents an incisive

though fictionalized account of Frederick's youth in his novel about Frederick William I, *Der Vater* (Stuttgart, 1957).

7. Frederick reportedly deleted these lines from his *Histoire de Mon Temps* at the behest of Voltaire. See *Memoirs pour servir à la vie de M. de Voltaire* (Paris, 1945), pp. 38-39.

8. See Hennings, *Linken Hand*, pp. 216-21.

9. Pick, *Maria Theresa*, p. 75.

10. William Coxe, *History of the House of Austria* (London, 1882), III, 269-70.

11. Most English-language biographies are hopelessly romantic in discussing this situation. Crankshaw, *Maria Theresa*, is a notable exception, see esp. pp. 67-81. Pick is also worth perusing on this matter, ch. 5.

12. Duc de Broglie, *Frederick the Great and Maria Theresa* (London, 1883), II, 245.

13. See Goethe's autobiography, *Truth and Poetry*, especially Part One, Book Five, in which he describes the subsequent coronation of Joseph and therein refers to anecdotes told by his elders about the earlier ceremony.

14. Arneth, II, 563-64.

15. On Francis' financial acumen, see Hanns Leo Mikoletzky, "Franz Stephan von Lothringen als Wirtschaftspolitiker," *Mitteilungen des österreichische Staatsarchiv*, XIII (1960), 321-57; and Mikoletzky, *Kaiser Franz I. Stefan und der Ursprung des habsburgisch-lothringischen Familienvermögens* (Vienna, 1961).

16. C. L. Morris, *Maria Theresa. The Last Conservative* (New York, 1937), pp. 210-11.

17. For English attitudes toward the Italian campaigns, see Spenser Wilkinson, *The Defense of Piedmont 1742-1748* (Oxford, 1927).

18. On the English attitude toward Prussia, see Sir Richard Lodge, *Great Britain and Prussia in the Eighteenth Century* (Oxford, 1923) and D. B. Horn, *Great Britain and Europe in the Eighteenth Century* (Oxford, 1967), ch. 6.

19. On the Bavarian exchange (and Austrian policy in Italy generally), see William J. McGill, "The Roots of Policy: Kaunitz in Italy and the Netherlands, 1742-1746," *Central European History*, I.2 (June, 1968), 131-49.

20. Coxe, *House of Austria*, III, 318.

21. Kaunitz (1711-1794) was to become one of the most important figures of Maria Theresa's reign. He had first entered her service as a diplomatic messenger to announce the birth of Joseph in Italy. In 1742 he became ambassador to Sardinia. Called to the Netherlands in 1744, he remained there until 1746. After a brief retirement, ostensibly for reasons of health, he returned as representative to the

peace negotiations at Aix-la-Chapelle (1748), then served as an important member of the State Conference in 1749 and as ambassador to
France (1750-1752). In 1753 he became State Chancellor and retained
that post until 1792. There have been only three published "biographies" of Kaunitz and all are limited: Alfred von Arneth, "Biographie
des Fürsten Kaunitz. Ein Fragment," AÖG, LXXXVIII (1900), 5-201,
covers only to 1750; Georg Küntzel, *Fürst Kaunitz-Rittberg als
Staatsmann* (Frankfurt -a. -M., 1923) is exclusively political; and
Alexander Novotny, *Staatskanzler Kaunitz als geistige Persönlichkeit*
(Vienna, 1947) deals almost entirely with him as a representative
of the Enlightenment.

22. Adolf Beer, "Zur Geschichte des Frieden von Aachen im Jahre,
1748," AÖG, XLVII (1871), 15. Other standard discussions of the
Congress are the Duc de Broglie, *La Paix d'Aix-la-Chapelle* (Paris,
1892) and Sir Richard Lodge, *Studies in Eighteenth Century Diplomacy, 1740-1748* (London, 1930). On Kaunitz, see McGill, "Wenzel
Anton von Kaunitz-Rittberg and the Congress of Aix-la-Chàpelle,
1748," *Duquesne Review* (Fall, 1969), pp. 154-67.

CHAPTER III

1. Macartney, *The Habsburg and Hohenzollern Dynasties*, p. 116.
2. In this regard, see Otto Hintze, "Der österreichische und
preussische Beamtenstaat in 17. und 18. Jahrhundert," *Historische
Zeitschrift*, LXXXVI, 401-44. Cf. Friedrich Walter, "Österreichs Weg
zum modernen Staat," *Österreich in Geschichte und Literatur* [here-
after *ÖGL*], III (1959), 7-20.
3. Cf. Josef Redlich, *Das österreichische Staats- und Reichsproblem* (Leipzig, 1920), I; Otto Brunner, *Adeliges Landleben und
europäischen Geist* (Salzburg, 1949); and Albert Goodwin, ed.,
The European Nobility in the Eighteenth Century (New York, 1957).
4. Joseph von Hormayr, "Die Kaunitze," *Taschenbuch für die
vaterländischen Geschichte* (Munich, 1831), II, 9-103. See also Grete
Klingenstein, "Leo Wilhelm von Kaunitz. Ein Beitrag zum Bild des
Adeligen im 17. Jahrhundert," in *Bausteine zur Geschichte Österreichs.
Festgabe für Heinrich Benedikt, AÖG,* CXXV (Vienna, 1966), 121-37.
5. The standard treatment of the Theresian administration and
the various reforms it experienced is Friedrich Walter, *Die Geschichte
der österreichischen Zentralverwaltung in der Zeit Maria Theresias,
1740-1780* (Vienna, 1938). Adequate English summaries are W. L.
Dorn, *Competition for Empire, 1740-1763* (New York, 1940), pp.
42-52; and R. W. Harris, *Absolutism and Enlightenment, 1660-1789*
(New York, 1966), pp. 203-11.
6. *Politisches Testament*, p. 107.
7. A good brief account is Friedrich Walter, *Männer um Maria
Theresia* (Vienna, 1951), pp. 39-65.

8. Macartney, *The Habsburg and Hohenzollern Dynasties*, p. 118. Cf. *Politisches Testament*, p. 54.

9. Hanns Schlitter, ed., *Aus der Zeit Maria Theresias. Tagebuch des Fürsten J. J. Khevenhüller-Metsch* (Vienna, 1907), III, 71.

10. On Bartenstein, see Walter, *Männer*, pp. 19-38; Arneth, "Johann Christoph Bartenstein und seine Zeit," *AÖG*, XLVI (Vienna, 1871), 1-71; and Max Braubach, "Johann Christoph Bartensteins Herkunft und Anfänge," *Mitteilungen des Instituts für Österreichische Geschichtsforschung* [hereafter *MIÖG*], LXI (Vienna, 1953), 99-149.

11. Coxe, III, 189.

12. Guglia, I, 352-53.

13. Arneth, II, 565-66.

14. See Walter, *Männer*, pp. 123-46; and Frank T. Brechka, *Gerhard Van Swieten and His World, 1700-1772* (The Hague, 1970).

15. On Sylva-Tarouca, see Walter, *Männer*, pp. 167-88, and Egbert Silva-Tarouca, *Der Mentor der Kaiserin* (Zurich, 1960).

16. See e.g. Crankshaw, *Maria Theresa*, pp. 107-17.

17. Arneth, II, 195.

18. Macartney, *The Habsburg and Hohenzollern Dynasties*, p. 117.

CHAPTER IV

1. *Zentralverwaltung*. See ch. 3, fn. 5.

2. See R. A. Dorwart, *The Administrative Reforms of Frederick William I of Prussia* (Cambridge, 1953), and Walter Dorn, "The Prussian Bureaucracy in the Eighteenth Century," *Political Science Quarterly*, XLVI.3 (September, 1931), 403-24 and XLVII.2-3 (March and June, 1932), 75-94, 259-73. Also, F. Walter, "Preussen und die österreichische Erneuerung von 1749," *MIÖG*, LI (1937), 415-29.

3. Properly speaking, the term "provinces" is an anachronism at least until the 1760's, but it is used here for lack of a better equivalent for the German term, *Länder*.

4. Adam Wandruszka, "Maria Theresia und der österreichische Staatsgedanke," *MIÖG*, LXXVI (1968), 174-80.

5. Macartney, *The Habsburg and Hohenzollern Dynasties*, p. 120.

6. *Ibid.*, pp. 125-26.

7. The figures were: for 1739, 5,957,066 gulden, of which 2,088,533 came from Silesia; for 1763, 9,806,182 gulden. Walter, *Zentralverwaltung*, p. 255.

8. See Gustav Otruba, *Die Wirtschaftspolitik Maria Theresias* (Vienna, 1963).

9. See William Wright, *Serf, Seigneur, and Sovereign: Agrarian Reform in Eighteenth Century Bohemia* (Minneapolis, 1966), and E. M. Link, *The Emancipation of the Austrian Peasant* (New York, 1949).

10. Herman Freudenberger, "Industrialization in Bohemia and Moravia in the Eighteenth Century," *Journal of Central European Affairs* (January, 1960), XIX, 349.

11. Freudenberger, "State Intervention as an Obstacle to Economic Growth in the Habsburg Monarchy," *Journal of Economic History,* XXVII.4 (December, 1967), 493-509.

12. Arneth, IX, 261-62.

13. For the instructions, see Arneth, ed., *Briefe der Kaiserin Maria Theresia an ihre Kinder und Freunde* (Vienna, 1881), IV, 5-13.

14. *Ibid.,* p. 9.

15. Wandruszka, *Leopold II* (Vienna, 1963), I, 24-30.

16. Hans Wagner, "Der Hohepunkt des französischen Kultureinflusses in Österreich in der zweiten Hälfte des 18. Jahrhunderts," *ÖGL,* X (1961), 507-17.

17. Arneth, IX, 165.

18. Robert Kann, *A Study in Austrian Intellectual History: From Late Baroque to Romanticism* (New York, 1960), p. 116 and ff.

CHAPTER V

1. For the first of these interpretations, see David Jayne Hill, *A History of Diplomacy in the International Development of Europe. III. The Diplomacy of the Age of Absolutism* (New York, 1967 [originally published, 1914]), 500-33; for the second, Duc de Broglie, *La Paix d'Aix-la-Chapelle* (Paris, 1892); for the third, Max Braubach, *Versailles und Wien von Ludwig XIV bis Kaunitz* (Bonn, 1952).

2. Cf. *Politisches Testament,* pp. 87-88.

3. A valuable theoretical context in which to consider the deliberations of the Council is provided by F. H. Hinsley, *Power and the Pursuit of Peace* (Cambridge, 1963), esp. ch. 8.

4. Adolf Beer, ed., "Denkschriften des Fürsten Wenzel Kaunitz-Rittberg," *AÖG,* XLVIII (1872), 19-38.

5. For a discussion of Kaunitz's proposals, see McGill, "The Roots of Policy: Kaunitz in Vienna and Versailles, 1749-1753," *Journal of Modern History,* 43.2 (June, 1971), 228-44.

6. D. B. Horn, "The Origins of the Proposed Election of the King of the Romans, 1748-50," *English Historical Review,* XLII (July, 1927), 361-70; and Reed Browning, "The Duke of Newcastle and the Imperial Election Plan, 1749-1754," *Journal of British Studies,* VII.1 (November, 1967), 28-47.

7. For a recent view to the contrary, see Reed Browning, "The British Orientation of Austrian Foreign Policy, 1749-1754," *Central European History,* I.4 (December, 1968), 299-323.

8. Beer, ed., "Denkschriften des Kaunitz-Rittberg," *AÖG,* pp. 19-38.

9. L. Jay Oliva, *Misalliance: A Study of French Policy in Russia During the Seven Years War* (New York, 1964), p. 199.

10. Historians long ignored Russia's role in the crisis which led to the Seven Years' War. Herbert Butterfield criticized this neglect in his masterly essay "The Reconstruction of an Historical Episode: The History of the Enquiry into the Origins of the Seven Years War," *Man on His Past* (Cambridge, 1955), pp. 142-70, esp. 156-57. In response to Butterfield's challenge, Herbert Kaplan published his *Russia and the Outbreak of the Seven Years' War* (Berkeley, 1968).

11. Translation by Pick, *Empress Maria Theresa*, p. 157, from Carl Hinrichs, ed., *Friedrich der Grosse und Maria Theresia: Diplomatische Berichte* (Berlin, 1937), pp. 39 ff.

12. Fritz Arnheim, ed., "Das Urtheil einer Schwedischen Diplomaten über den Wiener Hof im Jahre 1756," *MIÖG* (Vienna, 1889), p. 290.

13. For details, most biographers cite N. William Wraxall, *Memoirs of the Courts of Berlin, Dresden, Warsaw and Vienna* (London, 1806), II, 358-68. Wraxall, however, was reporting anecdotes he heard on his visit in the late 1770's.

14. Pick, *Empress Maria Theresa*, p. 261.

15. Hennings, *Linken Hand*, pp. 360-61.

CHAPTER VI

1. See Hinsley, *Power and the Pursuit of Peace*, pp. 153-86, esp. p. 181. Cf. Friedrich Meinecke, *Machiavellism* (New Haven, 1957), pp. 272-339.

2. *Ibid.*, p. 318.

3. See Oliva, *Misalliance*.

4. Sir Reginald Savory, *His Britannic Majesty's Army in Germany During the Seven Years War* (Oxford, 1966).

5. F. Rebout argues that France, in fact, had reached an entente with Prussia about the western front, G. Hanotaux, ed., *Histoire de la nation française. VII. Histoire militaire* (Paris, 1925), 527. Louis XV himself still seemed willing to live up to the commitments made to Austria, but Bernis was nearly frantic in his conviction that France needed peace. See *Memoirs and Letters of Cardinal de Bernis* (Boston, 1902), 2 vols.

6. See e.g. Walter, ed., *Briefe und Aktenstücke*, p. 148.

7. On Daun see Franz-Lorenz von Thadden, *Feldmarschall Daun. Maria Theresias grosser Feldherr* (Vienna, 1967). Thadden tries to demonstrate that Daun was in fact a more capable general than the oft-praised Laudon. Daun's problem, however, was not incompetence, but excessive caution, and Thadden admits that flaw.

8. See Arneth, VI, 436-37, n. 149. On Maria Theresa's role, par-

ticularly in the critical years 1758-1759, see Dieter Ernst Bangert, *Die russisch-österreichische militärische Zusammenarbeit im Siebenjährigen Kriege in den Jahren 1758-1759* (Boppard -a. -R., 1971).

9. Arneth, VI, 332.

10. Friedrich Walter, "Kaunitz's Eintritt in die innere Politik," *MIÖG*, XLVI (1932), 37-79.

11. Zinzendorf had actually formulated the reforms of 1761, but Kaunitz had led the effort to enact them and so was most closely identified with them.

12. Crankshaw, *Maria Theresa*, ch. 14, esp. p. 230.

CHAPTER VII

1. See especially the volumes which Arneth edited: *Briefe der Kaiserin Maria Theresia an Ihre Kinder und Freunde* (Vienna, 1881), 4 vols.; *Maria Theresia und Joseph II. Ihre Correspondenz* (Vienna, 1867), 3 vols.; and *Maria Theresia und Marie Antoinette: ihr briefwechsel während der jahre 1770-1780* (Paris, 1865).

2. Morris, *Maria Theresa*, p. 176.

3. Arneth, VII, 103 and 510-11, n. 154.

4. Cf. Thadden, p. 176. See also Walter, *Männer*, pp. 7-18.

5. Joseph, like his mother, has had limited success in his biographers. The best are P. von Mitrofanov, *Joseph II. Seine politische und kulturelle Tätigkeit* (Vienna, 1910); Ernst Benedikt, *Kaiser Joseph II. 1741-1790* (Vienna, 1936); François Fejtö, *Un Habsbourg revolutionnaire: Joseph II* (Paris, 1953). In English, the best work available is Paul Bernard, *Joseph II* (New York, 1968), though Saul Padover's *The Revolutionary Emperor: Joseph the Second, 1741-1790* (New York, 1934 [2nd edition, 1967]) is of interest.

6. August, 1765, Arneth, ed., *Briefe*, I, 59.

7. Maria Theresa to Countess Enzenberg, August, 1766, *ibid.*, IV, 479.

8. Guglia, *Maria Theresia*, II, 233-34.

9. Arneth, VII, 163.

10. Letter to Ferdinand, August 15, 1765, Arneth, *Briefe*, I, 58-59.

11. Adam Wandruszka, *The House of Habsburg* (Garden City, N.Y., 1964), p. 145.

12. Fritz von Reinöhl, "Die Übertragung der Mitregentschaft durch Maria Theresia an Grossherzog Franz Stephan und Kaiser Joseph II," *MIÖG*, XI, *Erganzungsband* (Innsbruck, 1929), 650-61.

13. Arneth, VII, 62.

14. Arneth, VII, 187.

15. Reinhold Koser, *Geschichte Friedrichs des Grossen* (Stuttgart, 1921), Vol. II, Book 7, Part 4.

CHAPTER VIII

1. Maria Theresa to Maximilian, undated (probably April, 1774), Arneth, ed., *Briefe*, II, 322.

2. Arneth, ed., *Maria Theresia und Joseph,* II, 95. Friedrich Walter noted that this letter and four others from the same period are particularly important in delineating the differences and tensions between the co-regents. Walter, *Briefe und Aktenstücke,* pp. 390-91. Walter cited the letters of December 24, 1775 (p. 391); July, 1777 (pp. 408-9); July 5, 1777 (pp. 409-10); and September 25, 1777 (pp. 410-11). Walter translated these letters into German from the French originals published by Arneth, *Maria Theresia und Joseph,* II, 99, 157-59, 146-47, and 162. One should also include in this group a letter, probably written in December, 1773, which Walter translated (pp. 339-40) from Arneth (II, 27-28). Cf. G. P. Gooch's short but valuable study, "Maria Theresa and Joseph II," based on their correspondence, *Maria Theresa and Other Studies* (London, 1951), pp. 1-118.

3. Macartney, *The Habsburg and Hohenzollern Dynasties,* p. 98. Cf. *Politisches Testament,* pp. 28-29 and 101-2.

4. Charles H. O'Brien, *Ideas of Religious Toleration at the Time of Joseph II. Transactions of the American Philosophical Society,* new series 59, no. 7 (Philadelphia, 1969), p. 21, see pp. 13-22 generally. Cf. Wandruszka, "Maria Theresia und der österreichische Staatsgedanke," pp. 181-82.

5. Maria Theresa to Joseph, July, 1777, Arneth, *Maria Theresia und Joseph,* II, 158. As O'Brien points out, Joseph was no freethinker and sincerely desired the conversion of all his subjects to Catholicism (the religious training which Maria Theresa had prescribed had not been without results), but he defined the state as primarily "a secular institution whose ultimate purpose is the temporal welfare of its citizens. Religion is significant in public life only as it secures obedience to the laws and maintains public morality." *Ideas of Religious Toleration,* p. 21. The prince *qua* prince, then, is not responsible for the eternal souls of his people.

6. Maria Theresa to Joseph, July, 1777, Arneth, ed., *Maria Theresia und Joseph,* II, 157-58.

7. Robert Kann, *Austrian Intellectual History,* pp. 138-39. At present the standard works on the subject are Ferdinand Maass' five-volume collection of sources, carefully edited and annotated with lengthy introductions, *Der Josephinismus* (Vienna, 1951-1961); and two earlier monographs, Eduard Winter, *Der Josephinismus und seine Geschichte* (Vienna, 1943), and Fritz Valjavec, *Der Josephinismus* (Munich, 1945). The latter contains a helpful bibliographical review of nineteenth-century treatments, pp. vii-xvii. An excellent introduction

to the problem in English is Paul Bernard's "The Origins of Josephinism: Two Studies," *The Colorado College Studies* (Colorado Springs, 1964), number 7. See also Bernard, *Jesuits and Jacobins. Enlightenment and Enlightened Despotism in Austria* (Urbana, 1971). On Maria Theresa's attitude, see Friedrich Walter, "Die religiöse Stellung Maria Theresias," *Theologische praktische Quartalschrift*, 105 (1957), 34-47; and Maass, "Maria Theresia und die Josephinismus," *Zeitschrift für Katholische Theologie*, LXXIX (1957), 201-13.

8. His most elaborate memorandum on the religious question, the "Collecteana sur la puissance souveraine relativement à la religion" appears in Maass, *Josephinismus*, I, 335-89. For the above characterization, see Bernard, "Two Studies," p. 48. Maass, while he speaks of Kaunitz as the "philosopher of Josephinism," credits Franz Joseph Heinke with being the real author of the later reforms, cf. Maass, vol. III.

9. See articles cited in fn. 7.

10. Wandruszka, *Leopold II*, II, 116.

11. Macartney, *The Habsburg and Hohenzollern Dynasties*, p. 109.

12. Bela Király, *Hungary in the Late Eighteenth Century* (New York, 1969), p. 55. The best study of Hungary in this period is still Henry Marczali, *Hungary in the Eighteenth Century* (Cambridge, 1910).

13. Arneth, VIII, 494.

14. Arneth, IX, 316.

15. Maria Theresa to Joseph, September 25, 1777, Arneth, ed., *Maria Theresia und Joseph*, II, 162.

16. Arneth, IX, 360-61.

17. *Serf, Seigneur and Sovereign*, p. 54. Wright discusses the Raab system in ch. 4, pp. 55-70.

18. Payments were to be made monthly in cash, though after ten years cash payments could be translated into grain equivalencies. The decision to have cash payments was intended to ease the burden on peasants with smaller holdings who were more likely to be able to do wage work to obtain cash than to obtain grain surpluses on their own land.

19. On Sonnenfels, see Kann, *Austrian Intellectual History*, pp. 146-258. On his economic theory, see especially pp. 174-81.

20. Macartney, *Maria Theresa*, pp. 117-19.

21. For Kaunitz's views on education, see his memorandum of February 18, 1766, edited by Adolf Beer, "Denkschriften des Fürsten Wenzel Kaunitz," *AÖG*, XLVIII (1872), 98-158, esp. 100-107.

22. On Maria Theresa's educational principles, see Kann, *Austrian Intellectual History*, pp. 132-34; and Arneth, IX, 225-60.

23. For a translation of the General Law, see Ellwood Cubberley, *Readings in the History of Education* (Cambridge, 1920), pp. 473-79.

The development of the elementary school pattern, the most successful aspect of the program which the General Law embodied, derived from the Silesian School Code of 1765. Thus, ironically, as in the Haugwitzian reform, the lost province supplied the model for Austrian policy.

24. *Memoirs*, I, 298.

CHAPTER IX

1. "Anmerkungen über dermahligen Staatssystem des Wiener Hofes," September 27, 1764, in A. Beer, ed., "Denkschriften des Fürsten Wenzel Kaunitz-Rittberg," *AÖG*, XLVIII (Vienna, 1872), 63-74.

2. *Maria Theresa and Other Studies* (London, 1951), p. 56.

3. Interpretations of the first Polish partition focus on two general problems, the internal weakness of the Polish state and the aggressive designs of the partitioning powers. One view, popular among Polish historians who tend to emphasize the perennial Teutonic *Drang nach Osten*, argues that the partition resulted from Frederick's concerted effort to prevent Catherine from establishing Russian hegemony over Poland, with Maria Theresa, confronted by a *fait accompli* and pressured by Kaunitz and Joseph, grudgingly accepting a share. E.g. Hajo Holborn, *A History of Modern Germany* (New York, 1964), II, 253-57; and W. F. Reddaway, "The First Partition," *The Cambridge History of Poland* (Cambridge, 1951), II, 88-111. A second view maintains that the partitions resulted from the mutual and equal greed of Russia and Prussia, and that a desire for peace compelled Austria to participate. E.g. R. H. Lord, *The Second Partition of Poland* (Cambridge, 1915), pp. 45-55. An American historian has vigorously argued that both Russia and Prussia opposed partition, but accepted it to restore the balance of power in Eastern Europe overthrown by Austria's seizure of lands along the Polish-Hungarian border; see Herbert Kaplan, *The First Partition of Poland* (New York, 1962). Though Kaplan's work is the first detailed study of the first partition since Adolf Beer, *Die erste Theilung Polens* (Vienna, 1873), 2 vols., Albert Sorel posed a similar argument, *The Eastern Question in the Eighteenth Century* (London, 1898), pp. 262-64. Bernard implies the same, *Joseph II*, p. 78.

4. Arneth, VIII, 116 and 558, n. 182.

5. Cf. Saul Padover, "Prince Kaunitz and the First Partition of Poland," unpub. dissertation (University of Chicago, 1932), pp. 48-49. A portion of this dissertation was published under the same title in *The Slavonic Review*, XIII (January, 1935), 384-98. Lacy's biographer says, "It is assumed that Joseph was the driving force behind this undertaking; perhaps Lacy was as well." Edith Kotasek,

Feldmarschall Graf Lacy. Ein Leben für Österreichs Heer (Horn, 1956), p. 138. She discusses Lacy's role in the first partition, pp. 136-50.

6. Arneth, VIII, 391.

7. Cf. Bernard, *Joseph II*, p. 78.

8. The manner in which Kaunitz dominated the second meeting between Frederick and Joseph held at Neustadt in September, 1770, is indicative of his acendency in the government. For a lively, albeit fictionalized, account of the Neustadt meeting, see L. Muhlbach, *Joseph II and His Court* (New York, 1893), ch. 57-64.

9. Padover, unpub. diss., p. 105; cf. Arneth, VIII, 365-66.

10. Sorel, *Eastern Question,* p. 190; cf. Arneth, VIII, 595-96, n. 453.

11. Paul Bernard, *Joseph II and Bavaria* (The Hague, 1965).

12. Arneth, X, 796, n. 487.

13. Arneth, X. The entire letter to Joseph, dated March 14, 1778, is reprinted on pp. 371-75.

14. Arneth, X, 633.

15. See Max Braubach, *Maria Theresias jungster Sohn Max Franz* (Munster, 1925), especially chapter 2.

16. Arneth devotes only three pages to Austria's role in Revolutionary diplomacy (as compared with three hundred and fifty-four on the Bavarian crisis), X, 260-62; but there are two excellent summaries of the matter in English: Samuel F. Bemis, *The Diplomacy of the American Revolution* (Bloomington, 1957), esp. ch. 6; and Richard Morris, *The Peacemakers: The Great Powers and American Independence* (New York, 1965), esp. ch. 8.

CONCLUSION

1. Guglia, II, 383.

2. Emile Karafiol, "The Reforms of the Empress Maria Theresa in the Provincial Government of Lower Austria, 1740-1765," unpub. dissertation (Cornell University, 1965), p. 245.

3. Adam Wandruszka, "Maria Theresia und der österreichische Staatsgedanke," *MIÖG,* LXXVI (1968), 178.

4. Coxe, III, 481.

5. Wandruszka, "Österreichische Staatsgedanke," p. 179.

6. For a thorough review of the state of the Habsburg monarchy in 1780, see C. A. Macartney, *The Habsburg Empire* (London, 1968), ch. 1.

7. *The Holy Roman Empire* (New York, 1968), p. 249.

8. See letters to Maximilian and Joseph referred to in footnotes 1 and 2, chapter 8.

9. "Kaiserin Maria Theresia," in Hugo Hantsch, ed., *Gestalter der Geschichte Österreichs* (Vienna, 1962), p. 251.

Selected Bibliography

PRINTED SOURCE MATERIALS

ARNETH, ALFRED VON (ed.). *Briefe der Kaiserin Maria Theresia an Ihre Kinder und Freunde*. Vienna, 1881. 4 vols.

ARNETH, ALFRED VON, and GEFFROY, M. A. *Correspondance secrète entre Marie Thérèse et le Cte. de Mercy-Argentau, avec les lettres de Marie Thérèse et de Marie Antoinette*. Paris, 1874. 3 vols.

ARNETH, ALFRED VON (ed.). *Maria Theresia und Joseph II. Ihre Correspondenz*. Vienna, 1867. 3 vols.

————. *Maria Theresia und Marie Antoinette: ihr briefwechsel während der jahre 1770-1780*. Paris, 1865.

————. *Die Relationen der Botschafter Venedigs über Österreich im achtzehnten Jahrhundert*. (*Fontes Rerum Austriacarum.*) XXII. Vienna, 1863.

BEER, ADOLPH (ed.). *Aufzeichnungen des Grafen William Bentinck über Maria Theresia*. Vienna, 1871.

————. "Denkschriften des Fürsten Wenzel Kaunitz-Rittberg," *Archiv für österreichische Geschichte*, XLVIII. Vienna, 1872, 1-162.

CHRISTOPH, PAUL (ed.) [pseud.]. *Maria Theresia und Marie Antoinette. Ihr geheimer Briefwechsel*. Vienna, 1952.

HINRICHS, CARL (ed.). Otto Christoph Graf von Podewils. *Friedrich der Grosse und Maria Theresia. Diplomatische Berichte*. Berlin, 1937.

JEDLICKA, LUDWIG (ed.). *Maria Theresia in ihren Briefen und Staatschriften*. Vienna, 1955.

KALLBRUNNER, J. (ed.). *Maria Theresias Politisches Testament*. Munich, 1952.

LIPPERT, WALDEMAR (ed.). *Kaiserin Maria Theresia und Kurfürstin Maria Antonia von Sachsen: Briefwechsel, 1747-1772*. Leipzig, 1908.

MAASS, FERDINAND. *Der Josephinismus*. Vols. I-III. Vienna, 1951-1956.

MACARTNEY, C. A. (ed.). *The Habsburg and Hohenzollern Dynasties in the Seventeenth and Eighteenth Centuries*. New York, 1970.

SCHLITTER, HANNS (ed.). *Aus der Zeit Maria Theresias. Tagebuch des Fürsten J. J. Khevenhüller-Metsch*. Vienna, 1907.

Schüssel, Therese. *Kultur des Barock in Österreich.* Graz, 1960.
Walter, Friedrich (ed.). *Maria Theresia: Urkunden, Briefe, Denkschriften.* Vienna, 1942.
————. *Maria Theresia. Briefe und Aktenstüke in Auswahl.* Darmstadt, 1968.

GENERAL WORKS

Andreas, Willy. *Das theresianische Österreich und das achtzehnte Jahrhundert.* Munich, 1930.
Brunner, Otto. *Adeliges Landleben und europäischen Geist.* Salzburg, 1949.
Coxe, William. *History of the House of Austria.* Vol. III. London, 1882.
Dorn, Walter L. *Competition for Empire.* New York, 1940.
Gershoy, Leo. *From Despotism to Revolution.* New York, 1944.
Goodwin, A. (ed.). *The European Nobility in the Eighteenth Century.* London, 1953.
Hantsch, H. *Geschichte von Österreichs.* Vol. II. Graz, 1953.
Hazard, P. *European Thought in the Eighteenth Century.* London, 1954.
Holborn, Hajo. *A History of Modern Germany.* Vol. II. New York, 1964.
Mikoletzky, Hanns Leo. *Österreich während das Grosse 18. Jahrhundert. Von Leopold I. bis Leopold II.* Vienna, 1967.
Redlich, Oswald. *Das Werden einer Grossmacht.* Vienna, 1942.

BIOGRAPHIES OF MARIA THERESA

Arneth, Alfred von. *Geschichte Maria Theresias.* Vienna, 1863-79. 10 vols.
Bright, James F. *Maria Theresa.* New York, 1897.
Crankshaw, Edward. *Maria Theresa.* London, 1969.
Gooch, George P. *Maria Theresa and Other Studies.* New York, 1951.
Guglia, Eugen. *Maria Theresa. Ihr Leben und ihre Regierung.* Munich, 1917. 2 vols.
Kretschmayr, H. *Maria Theresa.* Gotha, 1925.
Lafue, Pierre. *Marie Thérèse, imperatrice et reine.* Paris, 1957.
Leitich, Ann T. *Augustissima: Maria Theresia, Leben und Werk.* Zurich, 1953.
Macartney, C. A. *Maria Theresa and the House of Austria.* London, 1969.
Moffat, Mary Maxwell. *Maria Theresa.* London, 1911.
Morris, C. L. *Maria Theresa. The Last Conservative.* New York, 1937.

PICK, ROBERT. *Empress Maria Theresa: The Earlier Years, 1717-1757.* New York, 1966.

REINHOLD, PETER. *Maria Theresia.* Wiesbaden, 1957.

DOMESTIC REFORMS

BEER, ADOLF. *Die Österreichische Handelspolitik unter Maria Theresia und Josef II.* Vienna, 1881.

KANN, ROBERT. *A Study in Austrian Intellectual History from the Late Baroque to Romanticism.* New York, 1960.

KERNER, ROBERT J. *Bohemia in the Eighteenth Century.* New York, 1932.

KLINGENSTEIN, GRETE. *Staatsverwaltung und Kirchliche Autorität in 18. Jahrhundert.* Vienna, 1970.

LAMPEN, ANGELA. *Maria Theresia und die Aufklarung.* Innsbruck, 1945.

LINK, E. M. *The Emancipation of the Austrian Peasant.* New York, 1949.

LÜTGE, FRIEDRICH (ed.). *Die Wirtschaftliche Situation in Deutschland und Österreich um die Wende vom 18. am 19. Jahrhundert. (Forschungen zur Sozial- und Wirtschaftsgeschichte).* Vol. VI. Stuttgart, 1964.

MARCZALI, HENRY. *Hungary in the Eighteenth Century.* Cambridge, 1910.

MIKOLETZKY, HANNS LEO. *Kaiser Franz I. Stefan und der Ursprung des habsburgisch-lothringischen Familien Vermögens.* Vienna, 1961.

OTRUBA, GUSTAV. *Die Wirtschaftspolitik Maria Theresias.* Vienna, 1963.

REDLICH, JOSEF. *Das österreichisches Staats- und Reichsproblem.* Vol. I. Leipzig, 1920.

WALTER, FRIEDRICH. *Die Geschichte der österreichischen Zentralverwaltung in der Zeit Maria Theresias, 1740-1780.* Vienna, 1938.

WRIGHT, WILLIAM E. *Serf, Seigneur, and Sovereign.* Minneapolis, 1966.

FOREIGN AFFAIRS

BEER, ADOLF. "Zur Geschichte des Frieden von Aachen im Jahre 1748," *Archiv für österreichische Geschichte.* Vol. XLVII. Vienna, 1871.

BRAUBACH, MAX. *Versailles und Wien von Ludwig XIV bis Kaunitz.* Bonn, 1952.

BROGLIE, ALBERT DUC DE. *L'Alliance autrichienne.* Paris, 1895.

————. *La Paix d'Aix-la-Chapelle.* Paris, 1892.

CASSELS, LAVENDER. *The Struggle for the Ottoman Empire, 1717-1740.* London, 1966.

HILL, DAVID JAYNE. *A History of Diplomacy in the International Development of Europe. III. The Diplomacy of the Age of Absolutism.* New York, 1967. (Originally published 1914.)

HEIGEL, KARL THEODOR. *Der österreichische Erbfolgestreit und die Kaiserwahl Karls VII.* Nördlingen, 1877.

HORN, D. B. *Sir Charles Hanbury Williams and European Diplomacy.* London, 1930.

KAPLAN, HERBERT H. *The First Partition of Poland.* New York, 1962.

————. *Russia and the Outbreak of the Seven Years War.* Berkeley, 1968.

LODGE, SIR RICHARD. *Studies in Eighteenth Century Diplomacy.* London, 1930.

OLIVA, L. JAY. *Misalliance: A Study of French Policy in Russia During the Seven Years' War.* New York, 1964.

STRIEDER, JACOB. *Kritische Forschungen zur österreichischen Politik vom Aachener Frieden bis zum Beginne des Siebenjahrigen Krieges.* Leipzig, 1906.

WADDINGTON, RICHARD. *Louis XV et le renversement des alliances.* Paris, 1896.

WAGNER, FRITZ. *Kaiser Karl VII und die grossen Mächte.* Stuttgart, 1938.

WANDRUSZKA, ADAM. *Österreich und Italien im 18. Jahrhundert.* Vienna, 1963.

OTHER WORKS

ARNETH, ALFRED VON. "Biographie des Fürsten Kaunitz. Ein Fragment," *Archiv für österreichische Geschichte.* LXXXVIII. Vienna, 1900. 5-201.

————. "Johann Christoph Bartenstein und seine Zeit," *Archiv für österreichische Geschichte.* XLVI. Vienna, 1871. 1-71.

BERNARD, PAUL. *Joseph II.* New York, 1968.

BRECHKA, FRANK T. *Gerhard van Swieten and His World, 1700-1772.* The Hague, 1970.

BRIGHT, JAMES F. *Joseph II.* New York, 1897.

DUFFY, CHRISTOPHER. *The Wild Goose and the Eagle: A Life of Marshal von Browne, 1705-1757.* London, 1964.

HENNINGS, FRED. *Und sitzet zur linken Hand: Franz Stephan von Lothringen.* Vienna, 1961.

KOTASEK, EDITH. *Feldmarschall Graf Lacy. Ein Leben für Österreichs Heer.* Horn, 1956.

KÜNTZEL, GEORG. *Fürst Kaunitz-Rittberg als Staatsmann.* Frankfurt -a. -M., 1923.

MÜLLER, WILIBALD. *Gerhard van Swieten.* Vienna, 1883.

NOVOTNY, ALEXANDER. *Staatskanzler Kaunitz als geistige Persönlich-keit.* Vienna, 1947.

PADOVER, SAUL K. *The Revolutionary Emperor: Joseph the Second, 1741-1790.* New York, 1934.

SILVA-TAROUCA, EGBERT. *Der Mentor der Kaiserin.* Zurich, 1960.

THADDEN, FRANZ-LORENZ VON. *Feldmarschall Daun: Maria Theresias Grösser Feldherr.* Vienna, 1967.

WALTER, FRIEDRICH. *Männer um Maria Theresia.* Vienna, 1951.

WANDRUSZKA, ADAM. *Leopold II. Erzherzog von Österreich, Gross-herzog von Toskana, König von Ungarn und Böhmen, Römischer Kaiser, 1747-1792.* Vienna, 1963-1965. 2 vols.

Index

Aix-la-Chapelle, Treaty of, 49, 78, 79, 106
Arneth, Alfred von, 16, 72
Auersperg, Princess Wilhelmina, 87, 88, 108

Bartenstein, Johann Christoph, 25, 29, 33, 47, 52, 58, 59, 62, 68, 75, 79, 82, 106, 111
Batthyány, Karl, 74, 75
Batthyány, Lajos, 74, 119-20
Bavarian Succession, 137-39
Belgrade, Treaty of, 29
Belle-Isle, Count de, 33, 34, 40
Bernis, Abbé de, 90, 92
Breslau, Treaty of, 40, 47

Carlo Emanuele of Sardinia, 39, 40, 45
Catherine II of Russia, 76, 84, 96, 97, 132, 133, 135, 136, 139, 143
Charles VI, Holy Roman Emperor (father), 15, 16, 17, 21, 22, 23, 24, 25, 26, 27, 28, 29, 55, 65, 77
Charles of Lorraine (brother-in-law), 46, 59, 92, 93, 142
Charles Albert of Bavaria (Charles VII, Holy Roman Emperor), 33, 34, 38, 39, 41, 42, 70
Choiseul, Duc de (Stainville), 90, 92, 93, 94, 133

Daun, Leopold von, 88, 92, 93, 94, 96, 98, 99, 106, 111
Dresden, Treaty of, 47, 49, 51, 78, 80

Elizabeth of Russia, 80, 84, 85, 86, 94, 96
Elizabeth Christina (mother), 16, 23
Elizabeth Farnese, 39, 76
Eugene, Prince of Savoy, 16, 21, 22, 25, 27

Ferdinand Karl (son), 74, 104, 107
Fleury, Cardinal, 33, 34
Francis Stephen of Lorraine (Francis I, Holy Roman Emperor) (husband), 21-26, 27, 28, 29, 30, 32, 33, 34, 35, 37, 38, 42, 43, 44, 59, 61, 75, 87, 88, 93, 98, 100, 106, 107-9, 110, 117, 120, 126
Frederick II of Prussia, 22, 33, 34, 39, 40, 41, 44, 45, 46, 75, 82, 83, 84, 85, 86, 89, 92, 94, 95, 96, 97, 106, 107, 109, 112-13, 131, 132, 133, 134, 135, 138, 142, 143, 144
Frederick William I of Prussia, 34, 63
Fuchs, Countess Charlotte von, 18, 23, 24, 94
Füssen, Treaty of, 41

George II of England, 34, 90
Grassalkovich, Anton, 44

Harrach, Count Friedrich, 47, 65, 66, 68
Haugwitz, Count Friedrich Wilhelm, 56, 57, 58, 59, 62, 63, 64-69, 80, 88, 97-102, 106, 111, 120, 121
Hess, Matthias Ignaz von, 128
Hochkirchen, Battle of, 94
Hubertusburg, Peace of, 97, 106, 112, 131, 133
Hungary, 15, 24, 36, 37, 38, 67-68, 74, 119-20, 128, 145-46

Isabella of Parma (daughter-in-law), 104, 111

Jesuits, 17, 18, 19, 73, 76, 117-18
Johanna Gabrielle (daughter), 74, 110

[167]